Journey To Joy

JOY

Inspiring Stories of Women
Who Follow Their Hearts
To Live in a Space of Joy

Powerful You!
PUBLISHING
Sharing Wisdom ~ Shining Light

Journey To Joy
Inspiring Stories of Women Who Follow
Their Hearts to Live in a Space of Joy

Copyright © 2013

The authors of this book do not dispense medical advice or prescribe the use of any technique as a form of treatment for physical, emotional, or medical problems without the advice of a physician, either directly or indirectly. The intent of the authors is to provide general information to individuals who are taking positive steps in their lives for emotional and spiritual well-being. In the event that you use any of the information in this book for yourself, which is your constitutional right, the authors and the publisher assume no responsibility for your actions.

Cover Design by Jodie S. Penn
Editor: Sheri Horn Hasan

Published by: Powerful You! Inc. USA
www.powerfulyoupublishing.com

Library of Congress Control Number: 2013905909

Sue Urda and Kathy Fyler– First Edition

ISBN: 978-1-4675-7027-5
First Edition June 2013

Self Help / Women's Studies

Dedication

*This book is dedicated
to you, a woman on a journey
of living a happy, joyful and purposeful life.*

Table of Contents

Foreword

*There are many joys. But none so great as the joy
of taking form. Because it is here that you can experience
the heart-swell of love for all that is...for all of Creation.*

When offered the great honor of penning this foreword, I happily agreed as it is a topic dear to my heart. I then meditated with this request: "Teach me of the nature of Joy." Above is the first of many inspirations I received.

This book is clearly a blessed endeavor. The moment I entered this project, I have been on a most delicious 'joyride', as many "invisible helping hands" have intervened on my behalf. From mysteriously pulling up a webpage I didn't select and providing the exact quote I wanted in seconds to extraordinary wild animal and spirit visitations appearing whenever I asked for clarity, this very writing about joy has been a truly magical transformational journey unto itself.

It began when I decided that I could not, in all integrity and authenticity for all who read this, write a foreword to a book called "Journey to Joy" unless I was, well, joyful! Furthermore, I made the extremely bold intention that it would be a literal *transmission* of the frequency of Joy.

While I often do feel many levels of happiness and I even teach energy techniques that raise our vibrations into these higher states, this posed quite a dilemma for the part of me that still stresses about writing and deadlines. Now perhaps I really set the bar way too high. "Will it be 'good enough?' What can I say that hasn't been said? Who am I to write about Joy when I am certainly not living it every moment?" You may recognize the drill.

So I chose to work on my biography first as it was shorter and hopefully easier. Immediately my mind went straight into how much I despised writing about myself. My ego-detector starts buzzing loudly and I cringe at how to possibly capture what I do, much less who I am, in 150 words or less!

Since I just committed to be in a state of joy throughout this foreword process, I decided I must stop tolerating all the old stories my mind was filling up with of how hard it is to write. Period. I moved to my blossom-filled screen porch and focused on the beauty and yes, *joy* I feel listening to the birdsong in my garden.

I consciously re-chose: "I intend that I am gifted the perfect words to capture the esoteric nature of being an intuitive healer." In record time I put the final sentence to paper and something clicked within—my bio felt complete.

Without skipping a beat, the primeval screeching of sand hill cranes pierced the soft spring stillness. They were very close and intensely insistent. I knew I must run to see them and grabbed my camera. At the edge of my property I spotted them across the street. However, at the exact same moment the neighbor's huge pointer saw them too. He began his usual insane barking ritual. "Rats, he is going to frighten them," flashed across my mind. But I caught it and instead pleaded inside, "please don't scare them away." The very same dog who barks at me every day fell instantly silent. Something was certainly up.

Unfazed by the dog or the camera, the sand hill cranes marched directly across the street in a beeline towards me. This NEVER happened before. Standing nearly chest high, these two magnificent cranes stared straight into my eyes less than a foot away. For a split second I remembered hearing someone was hospitalized when pecked by their powerful beaks. But the energy of the moment was so soft and so perfectly timed, I felt no fear.

After a few moments, they walked all around digging the earth for tasty morsels with their backs to me, indicating a complete feeling of safety. Finally I gathered my animal intuitive wits about me and asked directly: "Why did you come and call just then?" Immediately the response came *"To answer your call!"*

"What was my call?" I wondered. *"To know what you write is TRUTH; giving others the experience of the bliss of Oneness through exploring the human/animal spiritual connection. It is so REAL."*

With the deepest gratitude, nearly twenty minutes passed in this contented easy space together, hanging out like "birds of a feather." Finally, I left them to continue writing. I was keenly aware of how light and free and empty I felt...a quiet self-contained joy that seemed to spill over to the natural world all around me.

My mood permanently shifted from worry to wonderment of what may unfold next. My intention to shift my stress about writing and be in a state of joy was working! The magic continued throughout the weekend. When I wondered about the veracity of a concept I was fleshing out, the first hummingbird I have seen in months hovered at my office window. In Native American traditions the hummingbird represents joy! Later two hawks screeched and swooped low outside my window till I realized the connection - hawks are the messengers between heaven and earth. What a magical topic this Joy is!

Our dreams and aspirations, I believe, are seeds planted deep within our hearts to point us to our passion and our earthly mission. Or as Joseph Campbell states so eloquently in "The Power of Myth:" "Follow your bliss. If you do follow your bliss you put yourself on a kind of track that has been there all the while, waiting for you, and the life that you ought to be living is the one you are living... you begin to meet people [or sand hill cranes apparently] who are in your field of bliss, and they open doors for you."

Yet following one's bliss, as Campbell concurs, isn't merely a matter of doing whatever you like and certainly not just doing what you are told. It is a matter of **identifying that pursuit which you are truly passionate about and attempting to give yourself absolutely to it.** In so doing you will find your fullest potential and serve your community to the greatest possible extent. Perhaps most fascinating to me was that Campbell often felt, as I certainly do, that as you aligned with your burning passion there were "invisible hands" that miraculously came to your aid.

So as a young adult, when I heard the phrase "Follow your Bliss" it made total sense to me, though it was not necessarily what I was taught. It seemed like "study hard, obey your elders, and follow the rules" was more the dominant theme. But I knew innately if I wasn't happy, I was no good to anyone. So listening to my heart, no matter how challenging it would prove to be, was not optional for me.

I was always extremely moved by nature and especially animals of all kinds. In their presence I felt home—alive, playful, and accepted just as I was. It seems the dream that was seeded within me as a child was about animals, especially horses. So at the ripe age of two, I begged my mom for my own horse. Being a city-girl she couldn't relate at all and tried to put me off by promising, "Okay dear, when you are ten years old." Game on!

With missionary zeal, I was determined to work up the evolutionary scale so a horse would be the inescapable next step—we got fish, turtles, parakeets, gerbils, cats, and when I was five—our first puppy, Rowdy. The day we brought Rowdy home I turned to my mother knowingly: "You know what's next!"

At 14 my dream came true—amazingly we got our first horse, a lovely little thoroughbred nick-named Happy. I thought the name a bit corny and planned to change it. But we couldn't—it was clearly his name. Aptly named, from that moment on I was on cloud nine. All the related hard labor I had to do—muck out dirty stalls, carry heavy water buckets and hay bales, groom and clean tack, ride rain or snow daily—never felt like a chore.

The beauty of this teaching is you don't have to know where your bliss is taking you. For over seven years, as I watched my horse play and graze, the very sight of him would make me cry tears of gratitude. But who could have possibly guessed that my passionate love for animals would eventually blend so beautifully and uniquely into my intuitive energy healing and spiritual mentoring practice for the most fulfilling and soul-full work I can imagine?

After a workout I often rode bareback with just a halter and lead rope to the front lane, where all the lushest grass grew. Happy quickly figured out our destination and would playfully buck and race when I had the least control. But this one day, as I was asking him to go easy on me, he became so soft; he gently glided into a trot, then the calmest of canters. I felt so safe, so relaxed and delighted—and then it happened.

Time shifted into slow motion. Flowing in perfect rhythm and harmony with my horse, I was acutely aware of each graceful movement. We glided effortlessly and I felt every detail exquisitely— every muscle, every breeze on my cheek, every breath. We were no longer horse and rider. We were no longer two.

I distinctly recall having the oddly comforting thought *"I could die 'happy' now."* What a strange thought for a sixteen year-old, but I felt so perfectly complete and fulfilled.

This incredible slow-motion merge seemed to last for hours, but it was merely a few moments and we were at the end of the lane. Another rider was driving in just then, and I wondered if she had witnessed my miracle ride. At the barn, she asked me about it. Though she had seen me riding Happy every day for years, this time she said it was like "watching a movie, pure poetry in motion." Even she could sense that something very unique had happened.

Back then I would not have called it bliss or an ecstatic experience of Unity Consciousness or the Merge into Oneness like I might now. I didn't have those concepts. Now, as I look back, it seems I spent the rest of my life trying to re-create that extraordinary ecstasy. While I had many moments of the deepest love, gratitude, and admiration for Happy, that exquisite experience of blissful connectedness eluded me. I had mistakenly assumed I had to be riding a horse to get there!

Years later, shortly after my father died of cancer, it seemed the "invisible hands" put me in touch with my first spiritual teacher. During my first intensive on Abundance a swami asked: "What do you desire?"

Since spiritual seekers were supposedly detached from worldly desires, no one answered at first. Sheepishly, the responses came: A lovely house, a new job, a loving partner, a Ferrari!

Deepening the inquiry, he took each example: "Why do you want the lovely house, the job, etc.?"

The responses came: "To enjoy beauty, relax, not be lonely, feel safe..."

"And why do you want all of those things?" the swami continued to probe.

At the core of each desire, big or small, material or emotional, was the desire to be *happy*. Without exception. So he concluded, if the goal of all longing is to be happy, why not go straight for happy first? This simple question rocked my world. I could be spiritual *and* happy!

However, I quickly became frustrated during the meditation as I wasn't experiencing anything at all. Later, while driving home, my whole field of vision shifted. Everything within my sight was infused with a soft, fluid radiance. Enraptured, my body was bathed in the most sacred sensations. Trees and even blades of grass seemed to bow and wave in mutual appreciation and recognition. Even the asphalt road was not solid, but undulating waves of scintillating light. I had the deepest knowing that every particle of creation was conscious, radiant, and fluidly connected.

And the elusive journey to joy stepped up a notch. Now my spiritual and personal goals were clarified...it was not just about being a good meditator or having a great horseback moment; cultivating consistent and deep contentment and expanded consciousness became the brass ring.

So how does one go straight to happy, much less joy and hopefully one day ecstatic bliss? I spent the past twenty-four years unearthing the process.

I now understand that everything is truly energy, and everything including thoughts and feelings, has different frequencies or vibrations. We are like one big radio, emitting signals all the time though our mind and emotions, yet we were never told we have the dial and can tune into blues, or jazz, or classical.

Our primary task then is to consciously and consistently raise our frequency to better feeling vibrational states. Even when your emotions are quite heavy, you can quickly reset to higher states. One of my students had her first "Bliss" experience at one of my

Quantum Creating retreats. While she had been reading some personal growth accounts of these transcendent possibilities, she had never had one herself. In addition, her mother had just passed. While practicing one of the energy tools she entered a state of sheer serene joy that lasted more than twenty minutes.

And as my awareness grows, so too the experiences of joy and bliss continue to shift and expand. Now I realize the very *vibrations* of words can be connected to directly.

You, too, can grab it directly. State out loud: "I connect with the frequency and vibration of Happy." In this way you claim the experience you choose. Consciously. Once you feel it in your body it will eventually override other choices. The higher vibration always wins.

If you are having difficulty getting into it, simply remember a time when you were very happy—a walk on the beach, puppy love, a gorgeous sunset—and visualize it until you can feel the sensation in your body. Then you can drop the image and go "straight for the vibration of Happy." Happy is a stepping-stone to Joy.

Joy is a choice. It is a frequency or bandwidth of vibratory energy that exists both within us and all around us.

I am no longer content to just "follow" the bliss in the outer experiential way, though it was certainly profound and a worthy endeavor. I long to abide in my eternal true joy-filled nature and shine like the Sun, as Rumi the *ecstatic* Sufi mystic exclaims:

"A true seeker must transcend those joys and delights that are just the ray and reflection of the glory of God. He must not let himself grow content with such things, even though they are of God, come from God's grace, and are of the radiance of God's beauty, for they are not eternal. What we have to do, then, is become the Sun itself, so all fear of separation can forever be ended."

In the ensuing pages you will read how many contributors had the courage and clarity to listen to their hearts and triumph in all areas of life. Perhaps against all odds, they emerged ever stronger and clearer and "followed their bliss" to create lives of unmatched joy and creativity and purpose. You will see how moments of deep doubt led these inspired women to delve into uncharted personal, professional and spiritual territory to discover their passion, live with extraordinary clarity and consciousness, and place these new-found and hard-won traits in service to others.

Allow these heart-felt stories to lift you up and provide you with "satsang"—or, the company of truth-seekers, who are living the shining truth that joy is not only possible but our natural state and perhaps our divine birthright.

Like many of the authors herein, following my heart—while at times taking every ounce of courage I could muster—has proven to be the most rewarding, surprising, and redeeming road I could have traveled. The ability to ease pain and suffering, and share ever-deepening understandings of how to more easily attain higher states of consciousness so we can co-create our deepest dreams will count as the most precious of gifts I could not have known existed at the start of this journey.

Once again I dove inside to understand the nature of Joy more fully and was gifted with these gems:

All creation runs on Joy.
Joy is the vibration of the stars singing to the Universe
It can be quiet or raucous
But it is always felt in the center of the Universal Heart
Joy is the clarion call to Incarnate
For all Souls sing with Joy at the hopes of gaining a body
Creation is anchored in the foundational frequency of LOVE, but it
    moves in Joy.
Joy is love in motion.
It is the whisper amongst the trees
In the rose, joy is the fragrance.
The birds' song, the butterflies' fluttery flight.
Joy is the Bliss that is available in the physical realm.

And as often happens when I am pondering too seriously, the tone of my inner guidance switched to a lighter note:

You want the recipe?
2 parts Harmony, 1 part Bliss, a dose of Love.
And if all else fails, "Jump for Joy—it works!"

My deepest intention for you:
May you inhale the vibration of Joy that exists in all Creation. Call in this exquisite frequency to continually inhabit your being, Igniting your internal flame of joy ever-present in the cave of your heart, so you may become the Sun radiating your joy-light to all.

EnJOY!
Kumari
www.kumarihealing.com

JOY

Introduction

*When we gather in the name of creation
all things are exponentially multiplied.*

Storytelling is an art and a calling—any of the authors in this book will tell you this is so. There are those who came forth beautifully open and willing to go to the depths of their personal journeys, and others who came to their stories 'kicking and screaming'—even though, of course, they chose of their own volition to author with us. Interestingly, those who fought themselves the hardest along the way now find themselves grateful and content in the knowledge that they stepped forward to claim their inner selves, and unleash their hearts.

Often the simple act of stepping into the work is a pleasurable dance and becomes its' own journey to joy.

And so, herein lie the hearts of thirty-five incredible women—trail blazers in their own right. Some of them had no idea that they were writers until the title of this book and the opportunity to collaborate called to them. They were drawn by some compelling force to open to the truth of themselves. Now, on the other side of the writing process, they will tell you that they have put forth not only their hearts, but also the essence of some profound and pivotal aspects of their lives.

Other authors came to this project secure in their writing ability, but had never written about such deeply personal and heartfelt material—at least not with themselves as the subject.

Either way, each author decided it was time to help someone else through the telling of her story. Many of them wanted to tell of the ecstasy of their transformation or the happy story of how things can work out beautifully no matter the starting point. Others shared secrets that they have guarded for many years, and now, for the first time, will be 'coming out' with them to their family and friends because of the opening this book has created.

In each case they discovered that an energetic transformation occurs when one puts pen to paper (or fingers to the keypad) with the intent to reveal her truth. As you read each story in this book, you will be captivated by the very core of the emotion of the author, whether she is speaking of creating a business with her family, healing from some sort of abuse in her life, opening to her inborn gifts, or she is still finding her way to joy.

Being drawn to the title on the cover, you are undoubtedly on your own journey to joy. By simply picking up this book, you have already leapt ahead towards your destination, and as you flip through the pages and read the words, you will catapult yourself even further along this path. Why? Because we are all connected, and your desire and willingness cannot help but bring you forward. The only question is; *will you go forth with ease?*

If you are truly ready to be joyful, I invite you to open yourself up as our authors did when they wrote their stories. The inception of any new project–your journey to joy, for example–carries with it excitement, anticipation, and a sense of mystery for what is to be revealed. Participants feel their way through a project (i.e. this book) most likely the same way they do in many other facets of their life: Some with the mastery of one who instinctively knows her way; others tentatively and carefully waiting for specific instruction at every turn; and still others who playfully step in and flow easily with whatever comes along–never worrying or questioning, simply accepting what is.

However you choose to participate, so be it. We only ask that you carry on!

My wish for you is that you commit yourself to be aware of your joy, however great or small, wherever it shows up, and whatever or whoever is the bearer. Be faithful to your desire for joy in your life and you will find that it has been there all along waiting to be discovered.

With deep gratitude and love,

Sue Urda

PART ONE

Joyful
Awakenings

*"To love yourself as you are is a miracle,
and to seek yourself is to have found yourself, for now.
And love is all we have, and love is who we are."
~ Ann Lamott*

The Right Direction

Bonnie Druschel

"The great thing in the world is not so much where we stand
as in what direction we are moving."
~ Oliver Wendell Holmes.

In the winter my mother often sent my sisters and I to bed with
our coats on in preparation for my father's drunken state when he
arrived home from the local bar. So much turmoil ensued that, for
our safety, my mother ran us out the front door as he stumbled in
through the back.

The next morning, my mother would force me to hop onto my
father's lap, kiss him on the cheek, and tell him that I loved him,
and all the while his breath reeked of booze from the night before. I
hated that! Why did she make me do that? Was she that clueless?

Four years old, the youngest of three sisters, every night, scared
to go to sleep, I had nightmares. I saw dead people hanging from
ropes in my closet. My Barbie dolls always ended up looking
massacred, no hair, no boobs, no arms, and no legs—only the torso
existed intact. I had no voice. I could never defend myself. When I
tried, nothing came out.

I remember going to a friend's house in grammar school. She
had a bunch of Barbie dolls and I was amazed at how she treated
them—I couldn't understand why she combed their hair, cradled
them in her arms, and spoke to them so gently. *Why in the world is
she being so nice?* I wondered.

Everything was always perfect in my family—the way we dressed,
the manicured bushes outside, the clean floor inside, and everyone
loved my father. Only I knew it was all wrong. I was five or six
years old when, the morning of our family picture, I snuck into my
mother's professional hair salon in our house, grabbed her scissors,

and cut off my bangs. She calmly gathered the pieces of hair, taped them to my forehead, and—as if nothing unusual had happened—took us for our family portrait! Everyone looked *perfect*.

The Artist Within

Despite the emotionally repressive environment as a child, I managed to be a pretty happy kid. My mother's clients were always friendly to me—I even nicknamed one of them my "fairy godmother" because she brought me gifts. I spent a lot of time playing by myself outside in the woods or in the fields on my father's parents' farm. My grandparents lived next door, first generation Poles and very strict. I cherished my grandmother on my mother's side—always so loving to me, she is still a warm and wonderful influence in my life.

I did ok in school, but hated it. In high school I was an athlete; it felt good to be in shape and to sweat, and sports was a way to prove I was *somebody*. I worked in the fields at my grandparent's farm—hard work and discipline seemed to follow me wherever I went, and it made me feel accomplished on some level.

I fell into a crowd in high school that liked to party, hang out, drink, and smoke pot. A small town girl, I didn't think much about it—it was just what I did. Eventually, I developed a reputation for being with one guy one week, and another the next. I wasn't the only one, but somehow I got labeled while the others didn't. Naive, I didn't realize then I was simply looking for someone to love me.

At seventeen I took an art class at a vocational school and realized how it made me feel—like I had some talent, like I was something or someone special! I loved being there, painting the still life scene set up by the teacher...I decided then that I wanted to be an artist, but had no clue how to make that happen.

I attended community college, but that lasted all of one month. At eighteen, somehow I landed a job in the athletic department at a local university. At the age of twenty, although I knew nothing about the law of attraction, I wrote down on a piece of paper the qualities I wanted in a man: funny, nice, cute, educated, playful, and loving. Later that year, invited by a high school friend to visit him in New York City, I was greeted at the door by his roommate, Tom. The nicest guy, I discovered Tom matched everything on my list! Engaged to be married within six months, I moved to New York to be with him and attend business school. I followed my heart and, two years later, we married.

Creative Healing

A few years after that we moved from New York to the Boston area to be closer to my mother, who now cared for my father, recently diagnosed with Alzheimer's. I not only worked full-time at a Fortune 500 company, but attended college full-time as well. After finishing my Associates Degree in Business we moved back to western Massachusetts.

One day during a routine gynecological appointment, the doctor discovered a cyst the size of a grapefruit on my ovary. I rushed to get a second opinion. What should have been an easy in and out operation turned into major reconstruction of my ovaries, as they pulled out my guts and put back them together again. Turns out, I was really sick and didn't know it!

What's going on? I wondered. *Why the hell is this happening to me? What am I doing? What's this all about?*

Then my sister gave me Louise Hay's book "You Can Heal Your Life" as a get well gift, and I began to answer my own questions. Soon, this book became my bible and launched my twenty-year journey into spirituality and full creative healing.

The path to becoming my full creative self was gradual and persistent. Eventually I learned that the site of my injury resided within my second chakra—a strong indication of repressed creativity! I realized I had layer upon layer of emotional blocks and hurts locked deep inside.

I began to apply new, more positive concepts to my life, and things began to shift. I felt better and took better care of myself—got myself into therapy, started practicing meditation, improved my diet, and began exercising again. I could feel some of the shame melting away.

At about the same time, I decided to allow myself to do something I loved and enrolled in an art class as an elective. Hours would go by seamlessly when I had a paintbrush in my hand! All I knew is that when I painted, it made me feel really good, and making art became the only thing I wanted to do.

I decided to go for my dream—I applied to the University of Massachusetts at Amherst and was accepted into the art department! We moved back to my hometown and I began to live my dream of becoming an artist. Immediately the tape in my head began to say "art is a stupid career choice!" I didn't care. I had to do it! Everything would work out somehow...

The Art of Forgiveness

In her book, Louise Hay states that all "dis-ease" comes from a state of un-forgiveness, and this resonated strongly with me. She also writes that the very person you find it hardest to forgive is the one you need to let go of the most. When I realized I'd never completely forgiven my parents, I began to practice forgiving and releasing. I knew I needed to stop seeking approval from others, and build greater self-acceptance. In doing so, I began to release my internal critic and remove myself from toxic relationships.

Shortly afterward, all of this deep shame about sleeping around in my teen years came bubbling up from inside of me, and I realized my low level of self-esteem. I remembered some nasty comments boys had made to me, and in a flash, a memory surfaced: In high school I was invited to my first bon fire—the peer pressure was on.

The girl I got a ride with abandoned me at the party. I asked the other girls I barely knew if I could have a ride home with them, but they laughed at me and said "sorry our car is full!" I was the only girl left standing around the fire with eight guys...in the mountains, ten miles from home! I had to ask a guy I barely knew for a ride home. He took me home, and nothing happened.

So much pent up rage surfaced—I painted frantically on huge nine-foot canvases, I beat pillows fearlessly, I spoke up for myself! It was the hardest thing to do, and much of it came out as screaming, but my voice was finally being heard! I had to plow through negativity with positive statements and recondition my mind.

Early on, when negative feelings surfaced, I'd reach for a cigarette or a sweet treat. Now, I allowed myself to *feel* my feelings, to say "I love you" to painful memories that surfaced. Over time, I realized that to make art that resonates with others, I had to access experiences and emotions that were locked deep within me.

Along the way, I tried all types of healing practices: Vipassana—the ancient Indian practice of silent meditation; sweat lodge ceremonies; medical intuitive sessions; and shamanic healing. Certain healing practices resonated with me more than others, and I learned to live in the moment, participate in personal growth seminars, practice affirmations, and connect with nature.

Today I feel so alive, happy, and free! I take one hundred percent responsibility for my life! I let go, let God, and trust that what is right and perfect will show up for me. Every day, I live in gratitude and always ask the angels for guidance.

My artwork has been exhibited in the United States, Germany, and West Africa, and appeared on mugs, votives, gift bags, journals, and jewelry sold throughout the U.S. and Canada. My story is included in Louise Hay's book "Modern Day Miracles" and this past June my photographs graced billboard-style screens on 42nd street in New York City. I've spoken at women's conferences to audiences of more than one hundred people, and coming out in the fall of 2013 is my first published book "Sunflower Adventure: Always Facing the Sun!"

Life is good and continues to get better every day! I've found that the present moment is where the power is and where creativity can flourish. I've learned to be who I am and to practice the art of forgiveness. I just needed to move in the right direction...

ABOUT THE AUTHOR: Bonaventure (Bonnie) has a love of nature inspired by a childhood spent in the gardens and farm of her grandparents. Her work is in collections and has been exhibited around the globe. Her inspirational artwork has appeared on mugs, votives, gift bags, journals and jewelry. Bonnie has a Bachelor of Fine Arts from the University of Massachusetts at Amherst and an AS degree in business and has worked at Fortune 500 companies. She lives in Western Massachusetts with her husband, Tom, and cat, L.G. ("Little Guy"). Bonnie believes nature heals, and it has always been her inspiration in art and in life.

Bonnie Druschel, Inspirational Artist
N.I.C.E. "Nature Inspired Creative Experiences"
www.bonniedruschel.com
bonniedruschel@comcast.net
413-427-7584

Hidden Gifts

Junie Moon Schreiber

I remember the moment when my father, diagnosed with brain cancer a few months earlier, was taken away by ambulance. Cut up, radiated, and changed, the man I leaned on and trusted—who'd been my champion and guide—was suddenly no longer there for me.

His personality had changed during his treatment, and he began sitting alone in dark rooms having bouts of anxiety about his mortality. He even made fun of me for things he used to admire. Overnight he became someone I couldn't trust. Much thinner now, he looked like my dad, but seemed like a stranger, and no longer represented someone I could rely on or a safe place to land.

My dad was everything to me—my best friend, support system, and a big hug at the end of my day if I'd been bullied at school. Not close with my mom, and feeling very alone in school, he was the king that reminded his princess everything was ok and that she was loved. I was fourteen years old watching my dad suffer, and all I could do was put myself aside and try everything I could to help him live. Only several months had elapsed, but the deep emotional pain of desperate loneliness took firm root, and I wondered how I'd be able to go on...

The day I saw him driven away and knew I wouldn't see him again, I changed. After those terrifying few months—with moments of hope that he would survive—he had a massive bleed and was gone. I remember that first day without him, as I lay in a fetal position on my bedroom's sheepskin rug asking myself how I'd survive. My dad was taken from me, and I blamed God.

Outwardly I remained the same—the bubbly, happy life-lover—but inside my trust in the world diminished. Trust that another could love and not leave me was shattered. Lonely, I decided consciously that I had to survive *alone,* and became Miss Wonder Woman who did it all and needed no one. How could I risk letting in other people? After all, I'd been harmed by allowing in my dad's love, so now I disowned the tender, vulnerable part of myself. Of course, what I also disowned was the beauty of letting love in.

Broadway Bound

After my father's death I focused on theater—I'd acted since the age of six, and as part of my new life after dad, I fully immersed myself in becoming a famous actress. Acting helped me connect safely to others without getting too close. It also allowed me to explore feelings without claiming them as my own—I could remain safe, as it was a character feeling grief, not me.

By twenty-six I was living the life of an actress in New York City, which meant I had a good job waitressing! By April 1990, I'd landed a role in a great Off Off Broadway show, was up for a role in an Off Broadway show called *Tony and Tina's Wedding,* and I'd just met Woody Allen's casting director and producer. My dream to be in a Woody film was possibly coming true as doors were opening and things were really happening! I'd worked very hard to get here.

Still, something was off. Desperately empty inside, my outside world looked quite nice, but inside I felt sad and alone. I was hurting and needed peace. I decided to attend a yoga class, knowing it would help me feel reconnected and whole. I left the class feeling alive and full and connected to life around me. What peace! Life was beautiful!

As I walked down 13ᵗʰ Street in my post-yogic bliss, I reached into my pocket, pulled out a cigarette, and lit up. Suddenly I stopped dead in my tracks. In that moment I saw myself at war internally. Part of me loved the excitement and thrill of being an actress— smoking, drinking, and staying out all hours of the night, waking up early to hit the pavement—while the other half craved a sense of peace and wholeness.

Suddenly I knew I needed to get out of the city, to step away and figure this out. I'd just finished a movie with Demi Moore and had a good chunk of money in the bank. I could leave for a couple of months and still pay my rent. *Where should I go?* I wondered.

There's No Place Like Home

Led to a magical place—a holistic educational center in upstate New York called the Omega Institute—I got a work position in the kitchen in exchange for room and board. The room, a tent, made me really happy. Back to nature, back to the earth...

There I met people whose hearts were full and loving, and experienced a sense of community like never before. Tears flowed down my cheeks at our first big staff/community gathering, because for the first time since I'd lost my dad I felt at home again. How odd to feel this way about total strangers whom I'd met only a week before! My eyes began to open and so did my heart...

Then one day, as I reached down to pick up something, I heard a pop in my lower back. Excruciating pain reverberated up my spine, and I could barely move. The pain was so debilitating I needed assistance putting on my shoes for the next couple of weeks. My plan to never ask for help or rely on others flew out the window, and I know now that we plan and God laughs! God had lessons for me and this was certainly one of them...

I felt such guilt staying there on an exchange program when I could barely move. They allowed me to stay for five weeks, and actually did whatever they could to make me feel at home and loved. During that time I rediscovered my connection to spirit, a peaceful heart, and a lifestyle that resonated. My world view changed, as did my way of life. My injury and incapacitation introduced me to different healing modalities such as massage, chiropractic, and energy work. I admired these healers and their lives. In fact, I wanted their lives! They were grounded, healthy, happy, and helpful people. I wondered if I could have that, too...

I decided ultimately not to go back to acting. Wow, that was big! My whole life, my entire identity, was about acting and being an actress. I believe strongly now—that the second I stepped onto the Omega campus—my back went out because the core of who I thought I was began to change. I remembered what life was about; that I am a spiritual being having a human experience. Healing began and so did my reconnection to spirit.

My decision to leave acting triggered the greatest loss I'd ever experienced—the death of my dad years before. I entered unknown territory once again and now my loss was that of my identity. Feeling alone and vulnerable, my connection to spirit also weakened. It was different than my dad's death but I felt the same—empty, alone, and in pain.

I know now with every ounce of my being that there was nothing wrong with my back at Omega, or during the years that followed. Even though my Omega experience brought me closer to spirit, the old wound of loss still festered inside. Still angry that my dad had been taken from me, this pain and resentment had bubbled to the surface and manifested as back pain and anxiety.

Looking Under the Covers

Though my life became richer and fuller after Omega, my back pain and anxiety remained. I knew there was still another piece to this life puzzle for me to heal, and thank God I found it in personal growth work. I began my next healing journey with an amazing therapist. Wow, did that shed light on so much!

Then I experienced Shadow Work®, a personal growth model that helps transform painful patterns to allow deep healing. It was here that my decision to become Wonder Woman at the age of fourteen was honored. It was explained to me that it had been appropriate for me to protect my heart from being hurt again because at such a young age I had no real tools for survival. However, during this process I was asked to look at how that decision worked for me now. I began to see how my self-protective behavior no longer benefitted me and that I was still feeling sad, alone, and empty inside.

Once I realized I still had deep pain despite my impenetrable emotional armor, I was ready to try something new—I grieved my dad. Boy, did I cry! I let it rip...and with the guidance of a great facilitator I shifted my perspective. Instead of perceiving my dad's death as a great tragedy where he'd been taken from me, I understood his gift of unconditional love. And I realized God had given me the best dad ever! God had wanted me to know this great love, so instead of hating God for taking my dad, I began to feel deep gratitude for the blessing of such a compassionate father.

My Tribute

Instead of closing my heart, I choose now to open it as wide as I can to honor my dad and all he taught me about love. I strive to be the loving person God intended me to be by gifting me the rich experience of my dad's love. Now my mom, to whom I was not close earlier in life, is my best friend. How better to honor my dad than to love his wife, who raised his children after his passing. Family was everything to him, and I love my mom now the way she so deserves.

I've come to realize that my journey toward love uncovered many treasures. I am not thankful my dad was taken, but I have gratitude for the journey. I used to be uncomfortable receiving, but now I've discovered what deep love truly is, and how it's touched my soul and changed my definition of love forever. When young and in pain I closed myself off to love and friendship, but my journey has taught me how to give and receive love.

Once a person mocked for my loud laugh, today I'm found in a crowd by the sound of my laughter, which flows freely and gracefully. Instead of allowing my feelings to immobilize me, I embrace life, love deeply, and allow others to love me back. My days are full helping others, leading workshops, speaking publicly, and creating healing communities for women. I desire to continue to uncover my buried gifts, and to grow into a life filled with treasures of the heart and soul.

ABOUT THE AUTHOR: Junie Moon Schreiber is passionate about life and enhancing the lives of others. Her challenges of pain and her gifts of transformation inspired her to become a Certified Shadow Work® Facilitator, Transformational Coach and Speaker. Presently, she is studying Tony Robbins Coaching Techniques at the Robbins/Madanes Institute for Strategic Intervention. She also is an interfaith minister and licensed acupuncturist. . Helping others with tools to embrace life more deeply and allowing joy in is Junie's heartfelt desire in the work she offers. For over 20 years, Junie has been in service to others helping people realize their truest potential to have magnificent lives.

Junie Moon Schreiber
Junie Moon's Soulful Expressions
www.theshadowworker.com
info@theshadowworker.com
973-874-0427

A Positive Mom's Fairy Tale

Elayna Fernandez

Tired after a long October day, the room was cold and dark but I couldn't fall back to sleep. Something was wrong, and when I turned the lights back on, I realized my husband Ben wasn't home yet and that it was later than I thought.

Alarmed, suddenly the one hundred and twenty-five square foot room in which we lived felt as big as an ocean. *Where is he?* I wondered, as doubt and uncertainty filled my mind. I had no way to contact him. He might have gotten stuck at work, but somehow I knew differently...

Frantic, I ran outside in my not-so-warm pajamas and scanned the street looking for his car. It wasn't there. Now in a panic, I returned to our room and realized Ben's clothes were gone! Then, I saw the letter—it had been right there the whole time. I read the words, as my heart nearly pounded out of my chest. I wanted to cry out loud and scream, but I couldn't gather the strength.

"By the time you read this, you will probably realize I've left, and won't be coming back," the letter read. A few days earlier we'd arrived in Florida after a week-long cross-country drive from San Diego to close on a new home and "live happily ever after." The closing never happened.

I had a thousand and one questions, but was terrified to learn the answers, and didn't want to wake my one and two year-old daughters, blissfully asleep in my bed. I hugged my little angels and thanked God they were safe and in my life. My breath seemed to slow as I held them tight, knowing they were worth all the pain, anxiety, and drama I'd endured.

Now I fell to my knees and curled into the fetal position on the cold ground. Pressing on my stomach, I sensed an unfamiliar emptiness there that spread like the worst cancer and hurt like no other pain I'd ever felt before. *Someone tell me this is only a nightmare!* I begged. *Tell me I'll wake up to my usual life soon and everything will be fine...*

I felt pathetic, knowing I'd been living in denial, forgetting who I once was and putting aside my own desires and sense of self. *What happened to the bold, confident, driven, joyful woman I'd once been? I desperately wanted to be her again, to drag her out of the deepest parts of my being!*

Then the flashbacks began to play in my head. Before Ben and I married, I lived in my home country, the Dominican Republic, happily surrounded by loving and supportive friends and family, enjoying a successful career. I *was* living the life I always dreamed about and for which I'd worked so hard. *So why had I given it all up for the man who'd just left me all alone?* I berated myself. *How could I have been so foolish, and how did I get so derailed from my deepest purpose?"*

With a deep sense of guilt, regret, and overwhelming fear, I wondered if I could have avoided this downward spiral. Maybe I wasn't loveable—maybe I'd never be. My thoughts turned to avoiding divorce, as divorce meant failure...my failure. I couldn't believe my marriage was over after only three years! At the age of twenty-eight, my chances for shame-free happiness were seemingly over.

"All Men's Misfortunes Spring From Their Hatred Of Being Alone." ~ Jean de la Bruyere

Alone, ashamed, and without a penny to my name, stuck in this one room "efficiency" without a kitchen, I didn't have a job or a car. I didn't even know how to drive! I thought it was a tasteless joke that Ben had left the girls' car seats behind. I was so angry I'd ever believed in and loved him, but my desperation and anger dissipated suddenly when I looked up and there they were—my two angelic daughters, peacefully asleep, without a clue how their lives had changed forever. I sighed in relief. They didn't have to know, at least not at this young age.

I thought of Roberto Benigni's Academy Award winning film "Life Is Beautiful" and smiled, remembering how a parent can make the most dreadful horrors seem like the funniest of games to an innocent child. *I can do that,* I thought, and immediately a slight feeling of hope rose from within. I realized I wasn't alone; I still had my most cherished treasures. In the midst of my dark agony, I found comfort in a vision of love. I vowed to become a positive mom, a healthy role model, and a source of happiness to my children. This meant I had to reset my life and reinvent myself at any cost.

The days that followed were the hardest. My non-existent self-esteem and my uncertainty grew as I found out my children couldn't leave the country without their father's consent. Going back home to my family was the only "Plan B" of which I could think, especially when "Plan A"—if only we could work things out—was never going to happen. I didn't even know where Ben had gone, or what exactly we needed to work out!

How does one raise two toddlers with no money, no support, and no resources? I wondered. Having always longed to be a career woman—I'd started my first business at age seven—I was surprised that it didn't feel remotely exciting now that I had to leave my children behind to do so. I really wished I could have it all. *Maybe one day...*

I sought consolation in my prayers and the scarce telephone conversations with my family and friends overseas in the Dominican Republic. I prayed fervently for miracles, and lo and behold, they began to manifest. First, in the form of confirmation that I was definitely not expecting another child (as I'd originally suspected), then in the opportunity to learn how to pass the driving test and actually get a driver's license and, finally, in the possibility of a family friend renting us a home even though I didn't have a job or any type of credit.

The move to Naples, Florida was bittersweet. Finally we had a place of our own and the promise of a fresh start, but the feeling of failure crept in more often than I care to admit. People said "it will all get better in time," but soon I realized time is no healer. I fought frequently with feelings of inadequacy and low self worth. My body became so weak and unhealthy that I went down to sixty-seven pounds, a low number even for my four foot nine inch petite body.

"The Way To Read A Fairy Tale Is To Throw Yourself In."
~ W.H. Auden

Always a warrior, I managed to juggle my new forty hour-plus job with house chores and caring for my babies after daycare. I thanked God for my job success and for coming close enough to making ends meet, despite the confusion that invaded me with emptiness and sorrow. I longed to stay home—or at least to spend more quality time with my toddlers.

One night during Christmas break, I felt blessed to spend some time reading to my girls. Reading to them always brought me such joy. In between fairy tale pages, I couldn't help but think that crazy notion once again: *What if I could have it all? Isn't that possible, even for a single mom? If Cinderella could have it all—why not me, too?* Exhaustion was indeed getting the best of me, I concluded.

After blanket tuck-ins, nightly prayers, and goodnight kisses, I abandoned myself to yet another lonely, sleepless night. Upset, I refused to believe a girl's happiness depended upon a Prince Charming. Furthermore, I refused to teach that nonsense to my daughters! I tossed and turned in bed and recalled my wedding day. Not your typical fancy gown and tuxedo ceremony, it had been more like a modern-day beach party. My smile had radiated the promise of a happily ever after now long gone.

Determined to find a believable, objective, no-nonsense approach to this fairy tale—one that taught my daughters the lessons of character and values, and one rooted in reality rather than erratic illusion—I composed my own Cinderella story! Pigheadedly, before the crack of dawn, I outlined five core principles:

Although not thrilled about her circumstances, Cinderella, allowed herself to dream of the royal ball, a prince, and a fancy gown...she had *vision!*

Cinderella learned to dance without a partner. She also worked diligently, as per her stepmother's orders, and certainly would have been worthy of attending the ball, even if she didn't exactly get there through her own efforts...she was *prepared!*

When her fairy godmother showed up, Cinderella could have dismissed her as crazy and told her to go away. Though not thoroughly convinced it would work, she believed in the possibility enough to listen...she had *faith!*

When her fairy godmother commanded Cinderella to find mice, a rat, and a pumpkin, Cinderella gathered everything her godmother requested, no questions asked. She didn't hesitate—she simply took action to make her dream come true...she proved *diligent!*

Tempting as it may have been to stay longer, Cinderella heeded the rules and didn't forget her promise to leave before midnight. It was this very action which led her prince back to her...she was *disciplined!*

I enjoyed teaching *my* version of Cinderella to my daughters and decided to create my own magical life each day by making these simple yet powerful principles my own personal roadmap on my path to reinvention...and to joy.

"Do What You Can, With What You Have, Where You Are." ~ Theodore Roosevelt

I rejoice every time I think of that pivotal moment of choice. My journey from then on involved a lot of courage, surrender, trust in the unknown, and the willingness to let go of my anger and resentment. I forgave Ben *and* myself, and recognized the blessing in what I originally perceived as tragedy.

Living proof that there's a way to move from "once upon a time" to "happily ever after," from "always juggling" to "always joyful," from "feeling stressed" to "feeling blessed," I know now that the journey is not only worthwhile, but magical and rewarding. Today I travel the world contributing to others' awakening, sharing *my* Cinderella story on stages both big and small to inspire moms who cannot see the fairy tale life God has created for them to live.

I've learned to look at myself as who I really was, to love who I've been, who I am, and who I'm becoming. I've experienced so much goodness and witnessed so many miracles, that I've gotten to know myself and my value at a deeper level than would otherwise ever have been possible. In a state of constant gratitude and awe for my many blessings, I now appreciate the lovely gift Ben bequeathed upon my girls and me: A positive mom!

ABOUT THE AUTHOR: Elayna Fernandez-Bare is a Positive MOM, Bestselling Author and International Speaker. As a Certified Guerrilla Marketing Master Trainer, Elayna is the creator of the *Guerrilla Positioning System™* (G.P.S.), teaching MOMpreneurs worldwide to increase Credibility, Visibility and Profitability™, while living with integrity and balancing their passions. Elayna has been recognized with multiple awards, including Best Marketer and Mom Entrepreneur of the Year, and is often featured prominently on national and international media. Elayna is the founder of The Positive Mom Foundation, a non-profit organization dedicated to promote Character Education and family unity. She is passionate about #Motherhood #Mompreneurship and #Motivation.

Elayna Fernandez-Bare
The Positive MOM Foundation
www.ElaynaFernandez.com
www.MOMtivation.com
www.facebook.com/positivemom

A Little Ray of Sunshine

Angel Calvosa

A sharp pain pierced my lower abdomen and I knew instantly something was very wrong. My life changed in the blink of an eye and my heart nearly stopped when the doctor said "I'm sorry, there's no heartbeat—you're miscarrying."

The days that followed were the saddest of my life. The tears came frequently and the pain in my heart was unbearable. I needed every ounce of willpower I possessed to rise each day, put on a happy face and pretend everything was okay. The few people with whom I shared my tragic news either abruptly changed the subject or nonchalantly told me "oh, that's so common, just try again!"

What is wrong with these people? I wondered. *Don't they understand this was a living soul inside of me? Don't they know you can't replace a soul like an old pair of boots?"*

With no help in sight, I bottled my emotions inside until I could no longer contain them, and then exploded with anger. I lashed out at anyone and anything in my path, blaming everyone and everything for my loss...but most of all, I blamed myself...

The Light

As the middle child growing up in rural Missouri, my older sister was funny, my younger sister smart, my other sister athletic, and my brother—well, he was a boy. No one ever called me funny, smart, athletic or talented at anything. However, I was a happy kid, and people always told me I made their day brighter by being in it.

"What a little ray of sunshine you are!" others frequently exclaimed. I decided long ago that's exactly what I'd be—a ray of sunshine. *Each day,* I thought, *if I can make one person's day a little brighter, simply because I'm in it, then that's enough for me!*

I always knew a great big world awaited me out there. At nineteen, with all my worldly possessions and five hundred dollars in my pocket, I set out to explore it! I had grand adventures, rubbed elbows with the rich and famous, moved from state to state and job to job, always that ray of sunshine wherever I went. I never desired to settle down, get married, or have a family.

While working at a company in California I met a colleague who would—ten years later—become my husband. Greg later told me he knew the day he first saw me I was the woman he'd marry. When he asked me for a date I politely declined, saying we worked together. I was the free spirit; he was the guy with the fifty-year plan, and neither of us was mature enough to accept the other's lifestyle. Instead, we opted to remain friends. What we didn't know then was that we were soul mates not yet ready for each other.

More than a decade later—years of exploration behind me—I decided I was ready. I wanted *"it"*—something different, stable— something straight from a Norman Rockwell painting. I yearned for the "American Dream": the house, the car, the husband, the kids, and the success. On Valentine's Day in 2004, as Greg helped me move into my new apartment, he playfully chased me around the couch and kissed me. Two years later we married.

We learned about Greg's opportunity to transfer to the East Coast, where he'd grown up, on our honeymoon. Although he requested the transfer three years earlier, we joked that the universe wouldn't let him have it until he finally married me! He very much wanted to go. As a real estate agent, I figured begrudgingly, *well, if he wants to go, there are homes to sell there too*! We settled in New Jersey in a Tudor style home with a pool (something about which I'd always dreamed!) Just as I imagined, the town was straight out of a Norman Rockwell.

In a few short years, I gained the husband, house, and car. Now, I wanted the success! I decided to wait to have children until my business was prosperous, and though I worked hard, the real estate market crashed harder. Determined not to let this stop me and, even with the deck stacked against me, I threw myself into selling twice as aggressively as the other agents. Still, I did not make more money than everyone else—only put in longer hours with little success.

Life became dark and my brain focused on all the self-defeating nonsense it could find. During this negative period, I discovered a book I bought years before but never read that introduced me to the "law of attraction." Barely into reading it, my business turned positive in an instant! I closed deals and won awards, despite the same stacked deck and a seemingly endless market decline. And it all came easily!

I realized then how I created my life's journey and was grateful for all I manifested in my life, both good and bad. How incredibly eye opening to learn I controlled my destiny! I was elated that it worked! Now I had the husband, car, house, and success too, but somehow still felt unfulfilled.

I decided it was time to move to the next phase—a child. I believed that if the law of attraction worked for my business, it could also attract a child into our life. Soon, we became pregnant and experienced the happiest day of our life together thus far. She was our law of attraction baby! Now I was getting everything I wanted and dreamed about—I was going to become a mother!

The Darkness

After my miscarriage, countless questions, what ifs, and whys enveloped my thoughts. *How could God be so cruel?* I wondered. *If through the law of attraction I brought this baby into my life, was I also then responsible for her death?* In my misconstrued reality—and despite my doctor's assurances otherwise—I blamed myself for our loss. It was inescapable. Nothing...else...mattered...

My anger raged against God and myself—I knew I had to make a drastic change in my life and my feelings. Two vacations offered brief moments of happiness and peace, yet still I felt so much emptiness. I wanted nothing more than to understand what happened and why, and decided to address my needs from a spiritual angle. I went on a spiritual retreat, connected with some very spiritually advanced people, read a lot of books, meditated, and practiced yoga, but the best thing I did was listen to and reconnect with my soul. It changed my perspective immeasurably.

I realized that before I came into this life I contracted with many others' souls. Some souls agreed to remain with me forever, some only for a short time. Always, these agreements enhanced my life, whether I recognized it or not. I may have made an agreement with another soul to hurt me deeply so that I could locate again the light with which my awareness had lost touch.

Still, I wondered how we know when these souls and agreements are occurring in our lives. I began to understand that—whether it was someone I met briefly who profoundly affected me or deeply hurt me, or someone with whom I felt an instant connection—all were souls with whom I had made agreements prior to this lifetime on Earth.

In addition, I recognized that there are actually three components to an event: The imagined truth of the event; the apparent or observed truth; and the ultimate truth, or what actually took place. In my case, I imagined that somehow my thoughts and actions caused a miscarriage. Of course, my observed truth was that I *experienced* a miscarriage. The ultimate truth is that I'd contracted previously with a soul to come into my life for a short period of time. This precious little soul, who stayed with me only briefly, forced me to stop and reexamine my life and where it was headed. Shocked, I stopped, reassessed, and learned how to hear my own soul's voice.

Mindlessly on my way to achieving the American Dream, I didn't notice how it became merely a treadmill—grow up, get the degree, obtain the job, marry the spouse, acquire the house and car. And it didn't stop there. Next I wanted to get the better job, have the kids, retire, travel, and—finally—die! That's it; end of story.

Or is it? Might there be more to life than this? Couldn't I do the same things but experience greater happiness, joy, and fulfillment? Absolutely! I needed merely to stop and listen to my soul's whispers; to find my true purpose. In doing so, I learned that—while the law of attraction is an absolute law and can be a powerful tool—using it without specific knowledge and understanding of my soul's purpose might bring about undesired results. One of those souls who agreed to do something horrible to me might arrive to jolt me back on track.

Now, when I feel unfulfilled, lost, or as if something is missing from my life, I recognize that it's my soul calling. No longer will I turn a deaf ear! When I hear the sweet whispers of my soul my new mantra is: "Stop, listen, and reassess!"

I don't know whether another precious soul will ever come into my life, but I do know this: The precious little soul who loved me enough to die for me so I might realize my own divinity will forever be etched in my heart...

Today, I finally understand we are one—all united in this life as part of the greater whole. Some liken it to being a drop in the ocean, others to a single snowflake amidst a heavy winter snow. I compare it to being a little ray of sunshine. The sun is a brilliant and ever-reaching display of light made up of many particulars. Each single ray of sunshine is part of the glowing light emitted from the sun. When darkness falls in one place, the luminous sunlight continues to shine elsewhere on Earth. Sometimes we shine brightly. Sometimes we burn dim. Other times we can't see our light at all, but still we are part of the sun's glow.

Through it all, my childhood decision to be a little ray of sunshine was never extinguished, merely dimmed by the challenges of my own rediscovery. I shine brighter today than ever, and shall remain true to my purpose as long as I listen to my soul.

My antenna is up, my senses are open and, the more I listen, the more of my soul's whispers I can hear and glistening light I see. I can say now with rock solid certainty that I am, always was, and always will be a little ray of sunshine...

ABOUT THE AUTHOR: The etymology of Angel is "Messenger of God." Angel Calvosa believes her name is no accident and endeavors to reveal, through her life and actions, that each of us is blessed, in a unique way, with a perfect ray of light to shine upon and share with the world. Angel's beliefs are influenced by the teachings of Ernest Holmes, Abraham-Hicks and Neale Donald Walsch. She is an award-winning Realtor, serves as co-facilitator of her chapter of *Powerful You!*, is Vice President of her Rotary Club and supports the cause to save and improve the lives of children around the world.

Angel Calvosa
Angel.calvosa@gmail.com
www.facebook.com/angel.calvosa
973-570-0388

Parenting on Purpose
Christine Marion-Jolicoeur

The three of us are clumped together in a heap on the cool tiles of the kitchen floor crying—it's been a long, miserable hour in a long, miserable day. Devin is teething, his little red face wet with tears and drool, as Liam, ravenous in the way only a jealous two year-old can be, screams "but I'm hungry!" And I'm exhausted from years of sleep deprivation, anxiety, and most recently the birth of my second baby.

"This isn't working," I say to no one in particular. I need to do something *now*, but it's so hard when they both need me at the same time! I take a slow, deep breath and an idea emerges—in a moment of parenting spontaneity I scoop up one screaming kid under each arm and zigzag around the room to collect what I need. Once I have everything balanced painfully in my remaining fingers, we head for the bathroom.

Accidental Parenting

In a lot of ways I feel like I was parented accidentally. It was a different time. I know my parents did the best they could with what they had, and since becoming a parent myself I can appreciate their sacrifices and worries on a whole new level. Growing up, I lived with so much silence and shame and things I didn't understand. I felt the weight of all these rules about what I should and shouldn't see, hear, and do, but no one ever explained what they were or why. So I believed there must be big scary monsters out there and that I needed protection.

Always polite and quiet, I worked hard and did everything I was supposed to do. But inside I was screaming. I didn't trust my feelings or the confusing world around me. I never thought to question the rules—instead I became ultra-responsible, hyper-vigilant, and a diligent little worker.

I learned how to hurt myself, because if you think about it, perfectionism is basically self-harm with a nice name. I spent all my time and energy trying to control everything, but I succeeded only in being tired, resentful, and disappointed. My hard work was well rewarded at home and in school. In many ways I had a lovely life and everything I ever asked for, but there was very little joy in it. On the surface, everything seemed shiny and in order, but I wasn't making healthy choices. I still worked and pushed too hard. I hated it and knew I didn't want to do that to myself anymore—or to my kids.

During my first pregnancy, I discovered the beauty of self-care. Sort of. It was more like I took excellent care of myself for the baby. That was the first time I felt really healthy, decisive, and empowered, even in the midst of being absolutely terrified. When Liam was born I slipped quickly back into my old patterns. Immediately and intensely protective, I was like a mama bear. Everything had to be clean and perfect. I vacuumed when I should have slept and chased the cats off the furniture with a lint roller.

By the time my husband came home from work I was literally so lost I'd take two steps toward the bathroom, then three toward the kitchen, then turn back to the bathroom, because I couldn't decide what I needed more, a shower or food. Some days I compromised and ate in the shower. I read so many parenting books, it was ridiculous. The stack of them would stand taller than a colorful plastic block tower. I've always been very serious, kind of a research geek, so I thought if I worked hard enough parenting would be easy and I could skip all the stress and guilt. Not so much.

I was totally unprepared for this! The push and pull. The love and hate. I'd look into my baby's bright blue eyes and think *I love you more than I love myself, but you're sucking the life out of me, kiddo...*I loved him, but hated what the sleeplessness, hormones, and constant worry did to my life, my relationships, and my self-esteem. I agonized for days about the tiniest decisions and scavenged hungrily for advice about the big ones. Whatever decision I finally made I immediately regretted, certain it would have some long-term negative impact on humanity. I didn't trust myself or my parenting skills and clearly I wasn't taking care of myself at all. Fortunately, it was impossible for me to maintain that level of distress for very long.

When I was pregnant with my second son I thought: *This is going to be way easier; I've done this before and already made the hard decisions, so I'll be able to relax and enjoy it!* In a way that was true; I was less frantic, but it still kicked my ass every day. I only had twenty-four hours and two arms, how was I supposed to get anything done when I had two kids on me all the time, even in the shower and on the toilet? At first, my goal was simply to survive. I kept us all alive, got the kids dressed and fed, and maybe found three minutes to myself to throw on some yoga pants, brush my teeth, and eat my toddler's leftovers. Every day it was nurse, diaper change, nap, snack, wipe up sticky stuff, potty, nap. Repeat. It was all about the kids.

My life changed completely the moment I became a mum, and then again when my second baby was born. I knew that bit would happen, and I welcomed it. But there was also a third time. When my oldest started his inevitable and relentless "why?" phase it really forced me to take a good look at my priorities. Why *do* we have these rules? Why *do* messes bother me so much? Why *did* I just say "no!" to that? It's hard to be questioned so often without being affected by it.

I was flooded (usually while nursing at three a.m., groggy and alone with my thoughts) by even bigger questions, and each one crashed down on me like a wave until I found myself drowning. What am I trying to teach these little people? What kind of parent do I want to be? And what kind of people do I want my kids to grow up to be?

I compiled a mental list of essential values and qualities then felt a familiar panic wash over me. I had none of these things. *How can I teach what I don't know? I've failed before I even started,* I thought, as I swallowed my tears.

My Mess Became My Message

After a few days of wallowing, I decided it was time to open up about these feelings and get some help. I spoke to my husband and other mums, and worked with a counselor and a coach. Initially, my goal was vague and not very realistic. I wanted to find a role model, someone to tell me how to be a better parent. But somewhere along the way (probably at three a.m.), I realized I still had it all wrong. I had to do this for *me*, not the kids, if I wanted to make real changes—ones that would last this time.

On some level, I knew I was doing a great job. Devin is smiley and easy going, Liam has always been a kind and helpful toddler, but I couldn't accept any credit for it. I was doing all the right things, but for the wrong reasons. I was serving up vegan organic fair-trade lunches with a side of disappointment and exasperation. No matter what I did it was never enough, *I* was never enough.

When I realized that the only way to teach them was to be a positive role model myself, instead of working harder, I started doing the hard work. With time and support I tackled some issues from my past. I was able to get out of my own way enough to see why, in one way or another, I'd been fighting the same battles for years.

Things started to get better when I decided to give up. I gave up attempting to be perfect, or better than someone else, and trying to learn "the rules." Then I gave in to how good it feels to take care of myself. I let myself play and dance and make a mess. I asked for help and learned to allow someone else to actually show up for me.

I now see that this process of embracing my own amazingness had been slowly evolving over years. But it was my kids that motivated me to make huge, sweeping changes in every area. I gave myself permission to do what felt right and made friends with vulnerability. I set daily intentions and got really clear about what I needed to focus on. I made non-negotiable appointments with myself and my husband. I cut out a bunch of extra stuff and started saying "no" to things that weren't helping me meet my new goals. I ate better and slept more. I relearned all the important things grown-ups forget along the way.

I made the decision to live and parent *on purpose,* to teach and learn from my kids. I took better care of myself so I could take better care of my family. When I think of the fragile person I was not so long ago, I want to go back in time and give her a hug and say: *Shhhh, just rest. Don't take things so seriously. Learn to play, make a few friends and some big mistakes. You're amazing. Trust me, I know.*

Joyful Parenting

I push aside the toothbrushes, and quickly throw together some nut butter and jam sandwiches on the tiny bathroom counter. The jars roll around the sink as I cut the bread into dinosaurs. Liam and I eat sitting together on the toilet seat and Devin watches us while he splashes happily in the blue whale bathtub and gums a plastic turtle. Not perfectly done, but damn I feel pretty clever in this moment!

"I'm not so bad at this whole parenting thing after all."

"*Why*, Mummy?"

"Never mind kiddo, just eat your dinosaur," I say with a smile.

My best decisions are the ones I make without thinking about them too much, when I trust myself and trust my kids. I'm so grateful to my boys for giving me the two best reasons to reevaluate *everything*, and for not allowing me to do anything less than make big, bold changes. My life may be a mess, but it's a beautiful, joyful mess, and I am so happy to be parenting on purpose.

ABOUT THE AUTHOR: Christine is a social worker, author, artist, entrepreneur, research geek and joyful mum of two amazing little people. She studied criminology, psychology and chemistry in university and has worked in social work for the past 10 years. Being a social worker by trade and research geek by nature, becoming a parent led her through self-reflection, analysis and confusion, and eventually out the other side to trust, clarity and joy. Raising little people is the best and hardest job she's ever had. She's grateful every day for the lessons she learns about how to live and parent *with* purpose and *on* purpose.

Christine Marion-Jolicoeur
www.joyfulyou.webs.com
www.joyfulparentingwec.wordpress.com
JoyfulYouCMJ@gmail.com

Joy Is Like The Rain

Laurie Morin

Terrified of everything as a child, in grammar school I often had difficulty falling asleep at night for fear I wouldn't wake up to see another day. That was the era when schools held fire drills and instructed us to hide under our desks for shelter in case of a nuclear war. I was a little too smart to fall for that—what good was a wooden desk against a nuclear bomb?

My parents sent me to catechism as a kid because they thought every kid needed a church. For me, attending church made sense of the loneliness and isolation I felt at home. My first thirteen years had been miserable. Painfully shy and brainy, I was a Goody Two-shoes with no friends. You know the one—the girl in the corner wearing ankle socks and a Toni perm on the first day of junior high.

My life looked perfect from the outside. Mom was President of the PTA and a Brownie troop leader. She also baked the best cookies in town. Dad played kick-the-can and miniature golf with my brother and the neighborhood boys in our back yard. But as the eldest and the only girl, I was expected to be perfect. While other kids hunted for chocolate Easter eggs, I stood there looking like a little doll in my white gloves and patent leather shoes.

The only thing that saved me was books. I would read a book a day, escaping to places where girls like Nancy Drew and Jo of *The Little Women* got to have adventures of their own. Even though I was painfully shy, I knew that someday I wanted a life like that.

My parents fought over just about everything—but especially about money. My father was the sole earner in the family and controlled the purse strings—my mother never even knew how much money he made. She got a hundred dollar grocery allowance that had to pay for extras as well—including milk money, birthday gifts, and visits to the doctor.

Holidays at our house often turned into tearful disappointments. I'd spend hours before Christmas looking through the Sears *Wish Book*, but was lucky if my stocking contained one toy amidst the oranges and underwear. I vowed at a very young age never to be dependent on anyone for money.

Going to church on Sunday provided an escape from my reality. I loved hearing Bible stories, especially the ones that involved sacrifice and redemption. It made me hopeful that I could create a meaningful life, maybe even find a little happiness. My favorite part of the ritual was the music.

I chose to attend St. Mary's High School in 1965, where I had a chance to reinvent myself and to come out of my shell. This was a place where it was actually cool to be smart and get good grades. I became a cheerleader, a class officer, and graduated valedictorian of my tiny class of seventy-eight. Here I found joy for the first time.

It was the era of the folk mass, and my high school choir made an old vinyl record that still sits in my parents' record cabinet. I especially loved a song called "Joy is Like the Rain," a gentle tune that evoked images of billowy silver and gray clouds floating across a peaceful sky "always sun not far away." For those few happy years at St. Mary's, that hopefulness mirrored how I felt about my life.

Good Girls Don't Go To College

Nobody gave much thought to what would happen when I graduated from high school. At that time in small town America girls did not go to college—they found a nice boy, got married, and raised a family. In training for that from an early age, I'd help my mother make sandwiches while my brother sat around the kitchen table playing cards with my father and uncle. My father taught my brother to fish and play golf; I learned to sew and bake cookies.

Despite being valedictorian of my class, nobody encouraged me to apply to college. When graduation rolled around and there was no marriage in my future, the nuns located a scholarship to Our Lady of the Elms College, an all-girl Catholic school.

My tuition was covered, but when I arrived I was told I needed one hundred dollars for books. I'd worked all summer to buy school clothes but had no extra money. When I told my mother, she advised me to ask my father for the money. Terrified—I knew conversations about money usually turned into yelling and tears—I mustered the courage to ask him that night when he returned from work.

"I don't think girls belong in college, and I'm not paying for any of it!" he replied with a withering look.

My mother managed to get some money from my father eventually, but that was pretty much the end of my days at Our Lady of the Elms. I dropped out after one semester, and tried to figure out what to do next. One thing I knew for sure. I was never going to have to ask someone for money again. That meant I needed to finish college and get a good job. The only way I could figure to do that was to work my way through, and that is what I did. I worked for a year, saved money, and went to school a year at a time.

Eventually I ended up in law school, and during my third year met a smart, handsome lawyer who shared my values and passion for justice. I met Bruce on an internship, and he pursued me with flattery and flowers. He was deeply unhappy and I thought my love could save him. He eventually left his wife and two year-old son, and we moved in together.

I created a picture-perfect life for us. We had a nice home and entertained often. The photos of our fifteen years together show lots of dinner parties and holidays full of happy, smiling people. There were some happy times, but much of it was an act. Bruce was angry about his childhood and conflicted about leaving his son. I walked on eggshells to avoid triggering his anger, but it pervaded our life together.

Our fights were not about money. They were mostly about driving. Bruce worked his way through college driving a taxi in New York City. He routinely yelled, swore, and berated other drivers as he swerved between lanes. When he pulled up aside a muscle car and gave the driver the finger, I'd fantasize about the guy pulling out a gun and shooting us dead in the middle of the street.

Of course, those were not the only times we fought. I got upset when he yelled at his son, swore at his mother, or went into a rant about work. Eventually I realized I'd followed in my mother's footsteps and created a pretty picture to cover up a home filled with anger and hurt. I wanted to get out, but I didn't know how to leave without being the "bad guy."

The first time I tried to leave under cover of darkness. I packed up my suitcases and left them in the car overnight, ready to move into an apartment in the morning. I woke up to find my expensive jewelry gone, and the rest of my possessions strewn up and down the street. At first, Bruce did not understand what was going on. When I finally explained it to him, he cried and begged me not to leave. I didn't have the heart to follow through.

I had given up my former faith in Catholicism years ago, but when things were especially rough, I'd duck into a small church down the block from where I worked and pray for help. I prayed that Bruce would leave me, or do something bad enough to justify my leaving. None of those prayers were ever answered, and eventually I realized that I would have to take the responsibility to hurt Bruce in order to save myself.

Recovery of Joy

Asserting my independence created space for me to stop pleasing other people and discover how to find joy for myself. Through coaching and working with *The Artist's Way*, I discovered pieces of myself I'd given up in pursuit of love and meaningful work. Whatever happened to the writer, dancer, and artist of my childhood dreams? In college I'd taken dance and creative writing classes, though I chose psychology as a major because it was easier to envision myself counseling people than being a starving artist...

I'd practiced yoga and meditation for years, and knew that most faith traditions honor and promote being conscious, present, and living in the moment—but I'd been too busy protecting myself to really experience what that meant. When my marriage ended and I started to recover the lost parts of myself, I realized the experience of pure joy came in moments of total absorption—whether with work, relationships, or creativity. I began to intentionally find space for those moments, and then be fully present to experience the joy.

That led to some wonderful changes in my life. Always I'd longed to live on the water, but dismissed it as a fantasy that did not fit in with my hectic life. When I decided to live in the moment, I explored places on the Chesapeake Bay within driving distance of my job in Washington, D.C. I now live in a tiny beach cottage so close to the water it feels like I'm on a boat when I look out my front windows toward the bay. I start almost every morning contemplating the beauty of the sunrise on the water.

I also discovered Nia, a movement practice that draws from martial arts, dance arts, and healing arts. When I took my first class, I experienced moments of pure bliss that took me back to the dance classes of my college days. At the age of sixty, I got my white belt and have been dancing my way to joy ever since.

Studying *The Artist's Way* and writing morning pages connected with the writer in me. I started blogging, writing a journal, and creating inspirational courses for people who want to transform their lives. I have turned that into my own business, where I feel empowered to create life just the way I always imagined it could be.

When immersed in the creative process, I feel connected to all of the joy and dreams I gave up to be "successful" in life. Finally, I understand the metaphor of the song "Joy is Like the Rain." Like the weather, life is a process of transformation. Some days bring sunshine, others bring clouds and rain. But through it all, moments of pure joy fall like raindrops—available to fill the well of longing and desire inherent in being human.

ABOUT THE AUTHOR: Laurie Morin is the founder of *Create Your Next Chapter* workshops and group coaching for women in transition. Drawing on the skills she has learned over the past twenty years as a legal educator, small business lawyer, and entrepreneur, Laurie leads her clients through a process to understand and appreciate where they have been, what they have learned, and where they want to go next. *Create Your Next Chapter* workshops inspire women to become their own heroines, plot their own adventures, and create the next chapter in their life stories.

Laurie Morin
Create Your Next Chapter
www.lauriemorin.com
laurie@lauriemorin.com
410-286-1069

Bringing Darkness Back Into The Light

Kathleen Plant McIntire

Furious when my Mormon mother told my atheist father she was pregnant, he insisted on an abortion. When she refused, he shoved her in their car, drove down a bumpy road, and tried to force a miscarriage. Not married long, he wasn't ready for children. She didn't miscarry. My spirit was resolute to come in, and my mother told me once I was born he couldn't help but love me.

My father was handsome, funny, and very smart, but had two personalities—like Dr. Jekyll and Mr. Hyde. He possessed a horrible temper—one minute full of life and fascinatingly engaging, the next he'd fly into a rage. We walked on eggshells never knowing who was going to show up or which one of us might get hurt.

My earliest memories include my father's verbal abuse. Often cynical and critical, he'd scream I was a "stupid little shit," and make fun of me. If I shared an idea he didn't agree with, he'd sneer and say "smarty pants, you think you're so smart." My father was also physically abusive to all of us including my mother. He burned her with his cigarette and kicked her at Disneyland when she wanted to buy us little gifts for souvenirs. She had no power in the relationship to protect herself or her children.

One Saturday my father and I were going skiing with my uncle Bud and cousin Debbie. That morning, not liking the way his eggs were cooked, my father backhanded my mother across the face so hard she flew to the other side of the kitchen, hit her head on the cupboard, and fell unconscious to the floor.

I screamed and ran to her, thinking she was dead. I cried and held her. She came to, looked at me and said "be a good girl—Uncle Bud will be here any minute—go get ready." I cried that I hated my father and wouldn't go.

"Please, be a good girl."

I gathered my parka, gloves, hat, and goggles. The car pulled up, I climbed in back with Debbie. I smiled and pretended like nothing had happened, but inside my heart was broken and aching. Good at smiling and acting polite, I shut off the pain and drama from my house each time I closed the front door behind me.

Shut down, I lost my voice, became extremely shy, never raised my hand, and barely spoke in class throughout my school years. I'd break out in a cold sweat if I even thought about sharing something and my heart raced—its pounding blurred whatever words I tried to formulate. It became easier to say "I don't know," even if I did.

Revelations

In 1996, a year after my dad died, I felt called to engage in the Hoffman Process. For one week you fully feel the pain from your childhood and ultimately experience deep forgiveness for your parents. Bob Hoffman, the founder, says everyone's guilty but no one's to blame.

While processing my childhood and relationship with my father, I began to cry violently and couldn't stop for hours and hours. Another woman in our group had been molested sexually by her father, and was having a very difficult time. I remember feeling so sorry about what happened to her. I was thankful for only verbal and physical abuse.

Having my voice restricted created limitations in my life. Hypnosis in my twenties gave me the confidence to speak freely and to succeed in business. Being president of a board of directors many years later I felt compelled to start using my personal hypnosis tape once again. That night as I slept a voice told me to throw this tape into the trash, as it was merely a band-aid. I needed to heal the cause.

An advertisement in a local paper about voice movement therapy called to me—what synchronicity! Never able to sing on key, all who tried to teach me proved unsuccessful. Around our fifth session, my voice movement facilitator Pamela noticed that when I tried to fight back tears I'd shake my head "no" ever so slightly. She'd seen me do this before she said, and wondered what would happen if I exaggerated this.

"Can you shake your head back and forth—hard as you can—while screaming 'no!' at the top of your lungs?" she requested.

I did, and burst into tears.

"What happened?" she asked gently.

Suddenly I was barely two years old and saw my father grab my hair and force oral sex on me! I couldn't breathe and thought I was dying. I cried out—maybe only to myself—but he wouldn't stop. Wow, what an image! I told Pamela I thought I'd made it up.

"No, it's real," Pamela informed me, adding that she'd seen signs all along. "Trust your own visions, and really love, nurture, and be tender with yourself," she advised me.

Out Of The Dark

I shared this experience with my mother and two younger sisters. My mother denied such a thing ever occurred—this couldn't happen in *our* family, she insisted, and told me "pursue this and it will kill me!"

My sisters believed I had a false memory and said they knew I wouldn't lie purposefully. Clearly this wasn't something I could talk about with them. I felt alone with this horrible memory.

After years of different healing modalities, what bothered me most was my inability to access and retrieve other, similar memories. Occasionally, I'd catch a fleeting glimpse of a sexual incident during a session with a healer. Some memories surfaced in 2005 doing Cellular Memory Release, but mostly these incidents remained buried. On some level I'd known for years, but couldn't *really* remember, and nothing concrete ever surfaced.

Then in 2009 I worked with Staci, a woman trained in somatic trauma release. When she worked on my body, I began to feel, remember, and release my stored trauma. What surfaced was unbelievable...

I was twelve years old in the early 1960's when a beautiful platinum blond woman showed up at our suburban brick home in a bright red convertible. Dressed in a peach-colored chiffon dress, a patent leather belt cinching her tiny waist, and matching high heels, she looked like a movie star. Her husband worked with my father and for some reason she was spending the weekend with us. She showered me with attention, making me feel so special. She sat next to me and taught me how to file my nails properly.

She wanted to take me to a party. I remember begging my mother to let me go instead of to my church event that evening. At the party she gave me a screwdriver to drink saying she couldn't taste alcohol in it. She revealed the real reason I was brought there when she held me so all the adults could have sex with me.

I could never quite remember why I'd been haunted by that night, but as this memory emerged while working with Staci suddenly it was as if my legs wanted to run and run and run—totally run away! I realized they'd been running energetically ever since! It's clear now my consciousness must have left my body during these abusive incidents. No memories exist in my brain—only in my body. I have an easy, natural pathway to the divine because that is where I went when consciousness left me.

Learning to stay present in my body and not hover above it—to be grounded—is what's proven hardest for me. I also learned how to *feel* so I could *heal* and be *real.*

Into The Light

In May 2011 I was invited by the Nobel Women's Initiative, an organization comprised of women Nobel Peace Prize Laureates, to participate in a conference about ending rape in war. Before attending, I flew to my mother's home. I truly believe transformation occurs first *inside* ourselves and is then reflected *outside.* I needed to speak with her about the sexual molestation in my life.

Mama, I need to set my voice free, I need you to be my ally and stand behind me—can you do that?" I asked.

"Yes," she replied, "tell me what happened..."

We stayed up late into the night while she asked me endless questions and listened with her heart. Then she looked me in the eye compassionately and told me she was so sorry.

Several months later, on my last day at a small beach in Mexico, I started feeling an incredible angst and didn't know why. Reclining in a lounge chair overlooking the azure ocean, suddenly I needed to touch the earth. I lay down on the hot sand and an incredible sadness engulfed me. I began to cry.

I recalled that in my mid-twenties an astrologer-numerologist had shared my chart in class and said I had something important to do in the world around my sixtieth year. My sixtieth birthday was only a year away, but after endless years, hundreds of classes, workshops, therapies, and modalities—and thousands and thousands of dollars—there I was on that beach, still *me*! I hadn't turned into that other amazing person I'd always been seeking...

Deep down the *me* that had been physically, verbally, and sexually abused since I was tiny_didn't feel worthy of bringing anything forth on our planet. I believed I needed to be a better person, speaker, writer—everything! I was on a constant mission to become that better person, who was always out *there*—outside myself.

I had a huge "aha!" The laws of physics say energy cannot be made into more or less. I could never be *more* than what I am! In that moment I saw I was perfect, I didn't have to be better or different. I saw that God/Source created me, and *all* is love. I saw how our essence, our light couldn't be corrupted. I could love myself like I loved others. There's nothing important I *need* to do. That belief had put such an incredible weight on my shoulders. Now I was free to simply love and accept myself fully!

Once again I remembered staring out the window in grade school wondering: *If we could distill everything in the entire universe down to one thing, what would that one thing be?* With crystal clarity, I knew it was love! Only love was real—all else was an illusion.

I know now that, of the seven billion people on our planet, one in three women will be sexually or physically assaulted. That totals one billion women. I made a verbal commitment at the conference in 2011 to share my story through writing. Love and truth are two sides of the same coin. Atrocities continue in darkness, in silence, and with lies and denial. Now is the time for our voices to be heard and to break this chain—to finally bring the darkness back into the light.

ABOUT THE AUTHOR: Kathleen Plant McIntire is a transformational teacher, speaker, and healer dedicated to bringing forth truth, liberation, and awakening. She is the author and creator of *Guiding Signs 101*, intuition cards. She is the steward of MoonBear Sanctuary, a 28 acre retreat center in Northern California. Kathleen leads sacred journeys with women to Ecuador, Guatemala and Peru. Her next Journey is to Peru. Kathleen produced the film *Mayan Renaissance* which recently aired on PBS. She was a delegate to Israel and Palestine with Nobel Women's Initiative and two Nobel Laureates. Previously Kathleen had a successful career in business, has lived abroad and travels extensively.

Kathleen Plant McIntire
Soaring In Light
www.soaringinlight.com
kathleenmcintire@mac.com
530-478-9577

I Choose Joy!

Laura Rubinstein, CHt

"Why are you always so negative?" asked my mom, as she drove me home from my job one summer. We'd been playing the "yes, but" game for a while—you know, the one where she says "what if you tried so-and-so?" and I'd reply "yes, but..." followed by a long explanation of why whatever it was she suggested wouldn't work.

What did I know? I was fifteen. This particular day, though, her question struck a chord that rudely awakened me to my own negativity.

"You know, instead of focusing on the fact that it's going to rain, and being negative about it, you *could* say, 'it looks like rain, but *perhaps* we'll be lucky and it won't happen.'" Her words (especially the word *perhaps*) hit me like a ton of bricks and altered our relationship completely. It also sparked in me the new possibility that I could access some positivity on my own that would come in handy as I matured.

An unhappy child internally, I always imagined the glass as half empty. Adept at finding the negative in *every* situation, I absorbed my mother's subtle tendency toward criticism as a child. I wouldn't say she was overtly critical, but somehow I picked up on the underlying complaints, internalized this way of being, and embodied it for most of my childhood.

I remember feeling totally depressed and so unhappy because I had no idea why I was unhappy and didn't know how to make myself happy. For example, twelve years old when my family and I traveled to Israel, there I was in the Holy Land and I couldn't sustain any joy! In my late teen years and early adulthood I filled journals with the angst and emotions around being stuck in unhappiness.

In eighth grade my history teacher approached me one day and said "why don't you smile more often? You have a beautiful smile!" I had no idea I didn't smile much, or that when I did anyone would notice. There were times when I thought I *was* smiling, but when I looked at myself in the mirror I saw my expression bore no trace of a smile! *How weird,* I remember thinking.

During therapy in my thirties, I discovered that something in me connected to my mother's sadness. My aunt, my mother's sister, passed away when I was a year old. In addition to my mom's sadness over the early death of my aunt, she was also—unbeknownst to me at the time—unhappy in her marriage.

It was as if I'd absorbed my mother's grief over her sister's death early on, and determined to unburden her of it on an unconscious level. My mother has always been a lot of fun to be around, and not a constant critic. Nonetheless, I'm sure her unhappiness came out sideways throughout my childhood and that is what I picked up on unconsciously. I guess because I loved my mother so much I took on some of her unhappiness, and these kinds of emotions made me susceptible to negativity and sadness throughout my childhood and early adult life. And this, in turn, resulted in my "nothing is ever good enough" perspective on life.

The Beginning of the Beginning

For most of my childhood I witnessed my parents' exchange of affectionate hugs and kisses, and what seemed like a happy marriage. The rug was pulled out from under me suddenly when they sat my sister and I down at the kitchen table and told us they were getting a divorce.

What? My parents never fought! At fourteen, I felt intense and utter shock at hearing this news. I'd never experienced anything so disorienting and upsetting before in my life! This was the first time I saw my father cry, and to this day my eyes well up with tears when I recall that heart-breaking moment.

Devastated, I nevertheless found myself moving forward. I believe now it was the day that opened the door to my awakening, as some internal innate resilience automatically kicked in. However, it took several more years to plow myself out of my low-level rut of depression, lack of self-confidence, and myriad insecurities as a hormonal and moody teenage girl.

One of the greatest gifts of the awakening/divorce was that I began to really connect with my father for the first time. When my parents were still together, he was always working and often disappointed the rest of us by not being available. He didn't show up for school events or help plan trips, etc., so I never felt like he was really present in my life; I didn't know him.

Once my parents divorced, he, my sister, and I had regular weekly dinner dates. Often I'd call him with my most personal challenges. He became my confidante and my rock. The one I'd cry to when upset, he always had a comforting comment or piece of wisdom to share with and encourage me. His compassionate ability to listen and his acceptance of my emotional state helped me move through many dilemmas.

"Work on the garden, Laura," he'd encourage me time and again. "That's all you can do." He gently and lovingly taught me through the wisdom of his words that working from the inside out was how to become stronger and—ultimately—happier.

However, despite his sage advice during the early years of the divorce, personal angst followed me through my college years. My emotions ranged from producing serious study-holic behaviors to my being at times completely emotionally distraught. None of my friends saw this side of me. I saved it all for the tear-stained pages I wrote on in my journals.

Emotional insecurity stewed within me constantly. I don't know what I would've done without my parents' phone support and the graduate student therapists at the counseling center. The front lines of my support, they got me through, though still I had to free myself from the lingering emotional pain that wove in and out of my life for days—or, in my case, for years—and clung to me like the lingering scent of cooked food...

All of my pain came to a head when the rug was pulled out from under me a second time in my life eight years after college when my fiancé chose to break off our engagement. This earth-shattering event hit me like a literal slap in the face.

Turn around, look over here, your life of joy begins today! I heard from somewhere deep within. Mind you, I didn't feel any joy. But in the moment my fiancé was breaking up with me, I knew it was right. I didn't fight it. I wanted freedom from the pain, and my breaking heart knew I had to let go of old patterns. And I couldn't do that from within the relationship.

Night after night I cried out the pain, wrote about my deepest desires in my journal, explored various spiritual practices, and sought out mentors. I took responsibility for finding my own joy and learned what loving myself really meant. Things began to unfold and slowly joy emerged.

First Class Joy!

Growing from darkness into light took many forms over the ensuing months and years. That innate resilience proved reliable once again. I began to discover things I liked about me that I had been denying for years. For example, I found that staying up late, multi-tasking, and writing all came in handy. New friends showed up in my life.

I remember the first time I *chose* to experience and feel deep joy. Hiking with a girlfriend on a glorious southern California day in Rancho Palos Verdes, I looked up at the bright blue sky, felt the warmish breeze, smelled the clean ocean air, and out of me came a squeal—a sound of utter joy, just because I could! It felt so good, taking conscious breaths, I did it again and again on that hike, and each time I felt greater happiness!

Could it be this easy to have joy whenever I want, just because I can? I wondered.

I noticed when I felt grateful and began to keep a gratitude journal. I paid attention to the generosity of those who flowed in and out of my life, and to the positive events that took place around me. Over the course of one year of this profound practice, my life transformed almost magically!

I found myself able to manifest things both large and small: Amazing things like a free first-class roundtrip airplane ticket; a piano; and an all-expenses paid trip to the Olympics! Even when I thought of something small, like a postman or someone to help fix my car, they simply appeared in front of me. What could be more delightful?

These life changing events have truly been a gift! I've learned how to create joy in an instant. Indeed, joy is at hand now any time I choose to slow down and appreciate the moment, see the glass as half full, say "perhaps," and play with a negative thought to change my perspective so that I don't get caught up in negativity.

Joy truly is a choice. When I take a breath and feel how good it is, I let it in—that's joy! To be completely honest, it takes vigilance and a conscious effort to choose joy over and over. But the experience of playing for no other reason than *choosing* to experience joy is exquisitely fulfilling. It brings into my life the kind of ease, peace, and fulfillment that I craved as a child. This reinforces my positive attitude toward life and reflects back even more happiness...all because I choose joy!

ABOUT THE AUTHOR: Laura Rubinstein is a Certified Hypnotherapist, Author, and Social Media Relationship Marketing Strategist. She created WomenInJoy.com, Social Media Blast Off System, and co-founded the Social Buzz Club. Throughout her career, Laura has optimized marketing strategies for 1,000+ businesses. She is the author of *Transform Your Body in the Mental Gym* and *Feminine Power Cards* (endorsed by John Gray, PhD of Mars Venus) which offer practical tools that allow people to make profound shifts in their relationships and professional life. Her writings are featured in a variety of publications including Women Living Consciously, Social Media Mags, and her popular TransformToday.com blog.

Laura Rubinstein, CHt
Social Media and Relationship Marketing Strategist
www.TransformToday.com
Coach@TransformToday.com
619-940-6569

Awakening Through Autism
Lilly Partha

"Honey, I'm pregnant!" I couldn't hide my joy!

"That's great." I ignored the flatness of my husband Jun's response on the other end of the phone. Later that day he asked if this was really what I wanted. Our two sons, four and six years old, were already a handful, he noted.

And what about my medical school plans? In the process of filling out my applications, I thought indignantly: *How dare you! I can go to medical school later! Who cares about anything else? God is giving me a gift!* Married for sixteen years at that point, I thought, *that's long enough for a husband to know when to be quiet...*

I wanted to get my tubes tied after my second son's birth, but wouldn't you know it, my obstetrician was one of the dozen in the entire country who didn't believe in performing that procedure immediately after birth. He advised me to come back six weeks later.

Yeah, right! With two little kids and an upcoming move to another state, I couldn't go back to the hospital, even for a day. I planned to get it done in New York when we moved there, but it never happened. Things happen for a reason, and often only in retrospect are we able to see the pattern.

My third pregnancy proved to be traumatic and difficult. By the end of the fifth month I was physically and emotionally exhausted. Still, I tried, mostly unsuccessfully, to keep up my strength and a positive attitude. My long journey into a deep, dark place in my psyche began at this time—mostly in my dreams. Often I experienced vivid and telling dreams of long gone lives, and the message was always the same: "Never forget that you and your baby are the chosen ones for this purpose..."

The doctor declared Atma perfect, and I agreed! I held my

beautiful Atma as he was handed to me, laid him on my chest, and thanked him for making it so easy. Only six hours of labor, nothing compared to the much longer labors of his brothers. We both fell asleep and somewhere in my deep slumber I heard supernatural whispers from another world, and saw an old woman who told me the time had come for my penance. I woke with a shudder and held Atma tight, promising him my eternal love and care.

Autism's Arrival

I considered myself very lucky. Calm and placid, Atma developed normally and met all of the milestones. At nine months he said his first word, "mama." Yet I couldn't shake the feeling that something was wrong. But whenever I mentioned it to Jun, he told me to be happy we were blessed with a calm child after his two very active brothers. Little did I know then that his first word would be his last for the next seven years...

The worst fears of any mother concern her children. At different times in history, we feared the plague, typhoid, or pneumonia. These days, it's autism. Like most mothers, I was in denial when my son was diagnosed at the age of three. *Oh, he's just a little slow,* I told myself. *Look how perfect he is, so calm and composed, unlike his super-active brothers. So what if he doesn't turn his head when others call him—he turns when I call him!*

When others expressed concern about Atma's lack of connection with anyone beside me, I told myself: *Hmmm, he does only respond to me, but that's ok, he's just shy. He'll talk when he's ready. Look at Einstein, he didn't talk until the age of seven, and I heard that James Earl Jones didn't speak until the age of twelve!* Still, I started various therapies for him right away.

Atma's diagnosis was the third reason in my life to abandon my medical school plans. Initially, I received a partial scholarship at Northwestern University, and was guaranteed medical school admission if I maintained at least a B average. Instead I studied biology and electrical engineering at the University of Illinois and for the next twelve years worked in various technical fields, studied and practiced healing methods, and eventually obtained a doctorate in homeopathy. Upon learning of my first pregnancy, I put aside medical school plans and instead studied acupuncture and oriental medicine.

After his diagnosis, we immersed him in six areas of treatment: biomedical, nutritional, behavioral, sensory, educational, and energetic therapies over the next several years. Obsessed with getting him to talk, what followed was an eclectic mix of corrective treatments. While some of my patients improved rapidly and began speaking, my son did not. I visited many other doctors of all kinds with him, thinking there might be an energy interference from me as a mother.

Nothing worked. Finally, at the age of seven a miracle took place, and he started to speak! A pivotal point in his development, once his speech came, his true personality emerged. Atma is now very social and devoted to his brothers. Autism is a complex and variable disorder, and we continue to help him with its presenting challenges. He responds well when the whole family chants or meditates together. Prayer is authentic energy, and a necessary tool to link with the divine healing power inside each of us. I recommend this practice to all of my patients, regardless of their ailments.

Descent Into Darkness

While my outward life was hectic, inwardly I began to slip into a deep, dark abyss that seemed to have no hope, no light. I floated in a paradoxical darkness that was empty and heavy at the same time, and filled with constant heartache. Was I dead or alive? I didn't know any more. I didn't want to see or talk to anyone about anything, so I cut off my carefully built social circle. It was all I could do to manage my home and work lives. I didn't know why I was alive, or what had become of my upbeat, unsinkable personality. Was I depressed? I didn't know. I was just numb.

Interspersed with this mostly dead mental state, I experienced episodes of rage and resentment. *Why me?* I screamed internally. *What happened to the perfect life I'd designed for myself? Why had nothing turned out like I planned? All the affirmations and rituals, were they really just stupid self-delusions?*

Once, alone on a secluded beach, I beckoned an answer from the roaring and all-knowing ocean when I screamed at the top of my voice: "Why?" I received only the thrashing of a mischievous wave.

One by one, my relationships crumbled until only a few people remained a part of my life. My family never understood autism, and we received no support from either side. One close family member even accused me of neglect, claiming that's why Atma was this way. How could anyone say this to a woman who had children after twelve years of unexplained infertility, and whose paramount interest in life is their well-being?

It never occurred to me to seek help. I thought I had it under control. *How can anyone possibly understand my pain?* I wondered.

And even if they did, what can anyone do about it, so why waste time? When pain is not processed, it gets converted into bad habits, and before long I found myself indulging in excess food and drink. This didn't last long and—like all pain—was a great teacher. Now I live with immense appreciation for my body and supply to it only healthful foods.

My one solace, my only therapy during this darkest time in my life, was my studies. My love of learning and desire to improve myself never diminished, and I continued to pursue higher studies and obtain additional merits and training.

Lifted by Divine Grace

Since childhood, I've had a routine of daily spiritual practices. At this point, they'd become only dry rituals, no longer imbued with authentic devotion. Still, every morning, I'd chant and meditate. Finally one ordinary morning, more than a decade after existing as a parched preservative, my inner life suddenly flooded with grace.

Was it a dream, a vision, or what? I still don't know. I've had many spiritual experiences in my life (these form the subject of a book I'm currently writing), but nothing like this! I was sitting on a round, red balloon, holding on to a pole, as I traversed the breadth of time and visited galaxies beyond imagination. I saw tribal dances, spectacular landscapes, futuristic space vehicles, planets bursting, new life arising, wars, famine, celebrations, peaceful times, animals, and beings of other worlds!

I perambulated through black holes, starry universes, and bottomless oceans. Simultaneously I found myself present in the inner chambers of an atom, and the ever-expanding space of all that is. I was everywhere...and nowhere. I was of everything, yet only a witness, detachedly observing every passing phenomenon.

I cannot say how long this experience lasted—a few seconds or a few hours. In an altered state for several days, during which I experienced bursts of joy so intense I prayed to the masters to bring it down, many truths were revealed to me. Most of them I'd read in books or heard in lectures, but now, the voice was from within, not someone else's. Gradually, my state of mind returned to normalcy, but the presence of grace, peace, and love never left me, and this presence continues to guide my awareness.

This experience taught me so much! I learned that life as I know it is but a transient bubble. Still, I must honor my presence here and follow my dharma (righteousness.)

I saw that all my suffering stems from a basic lack of acceptance of my own destiny and fate, and how my need for control causes problems.

There are no mistakes! I chose my circumstances as the quickest path from delusion to bliss. When I let go and accept everything as it is, I am being true to myself. I am not betrayed by God when things don't go my way. On the contrary, I'm given a chance to deny the power of anything in this world to act upon me, and I thereby maintain equanimity. I surrender to the divine shakti—the divine cosmic energy that flows in and through me and all else. This power enables me to have the supreme vantage point.

My only purpose is to love and be loved at all times. This is not a one-birth game, and the permutations that led me here now are too numerous to calculate. All healing begins with forgiveness. I can't change my past; instead I must accept it, understand it, and create a different present. The future will rewrite itself.

Within a matter of weeks of my pilgrimage through the cosmos, longstanding pains and heartache disappeared. Fractured relationships started to heal. Now, effortlessly aligned with the infinite, I awaken suffused with love and joy.

ABOUT THE AUTHOR: Author, speaker, success coach, and holistic physician Lilly Partha embarked upon healing and spiritual paths at a very early age, and has spent a significant amount of time in the company of mystics. Lilly possesses five academic degrees and numerous trainings and certifications in various types of energy medicine. The founder and CEO of two private companies and several online ventures, she serves as a board member and advisor on others. Spiritual masters declared Lilly a healing presence, and predicted she will help many achieve health, peace, and wealth.

Dr. Lilly Partha
Holistic Health Inc.
lillypartha.com
drpartha@holistichealthchicago.com
630-737-1970

Owning My Joy

Sue Urda

I stand tall, breathe in deeply through my nostrils, and exhale slowly a steady stream of air through slightly parted lips. Hands together at my waist, I tap my fingers and thumbs together lightly to create a connection between my brain and heart, and to stimulate energy from deep within my belly. A gentle smile crosses my face. The ritual is in process.

Waiting in the wings to speak in front of an audience of beautiful, intelligent, and powerful women on the topic of "Conscious Connections," I consider myself lucky and blessed. Who would've thunk?

Not too many years ago I lived a disconnected life. Sure, from the outside my situation looked all rosy and peachy, but that's what I wanted everyone to think! Inside I felt as if I was dying a little every day. I owned a beautiful home that I loved, was in a wonderful committed relationship, had friends I enjoyed and to whom I was close, and co-owned and ran a growing business. My mom, sisters and brothers, nieces and nephews were all healthy and basically happy, but my physical body was messing with me. And finances—well, they were often a source of worry...

On the outside my life looked pretty good, but inside I felt like I was drowning...which was ironic, because the times I felt most alive were when I drowned my pain, discomfort, and angst in a hot tub as I soaked in Epsom salts and lavender oil. Meditative music playing in the background—I can hear it even now—was accompanied by positive affirmations recorded in my own voice. These affirmations talked about how I wanted to heal my body, create abundance, be "healthy and vibrant and strong, sexy and happy and rich," and live in freedom and joy...

Joy—there was that word again, and it brought me abruptly back to the present.

Life was moving along nicely and things had come around for me. Speaking so comfortably in front of these women was evidence to me that I'd turned a corner. And then I heard it...

"She's an inspirational leader, a powerful speaker, consummate student, and joyful woman," said my partner Kathy as she introduced me to the audience.

What—a joyful woman? Suddenly disconcerted, the words struck like a blow deep to my gut and literally took away my breath. *Is she really talking about me? Who wrote that introduction anyway? Oh yeah...it was me...*

I regain my composure, plant the smile back on my lips, and remind myself of the ritual. Ah yes. The ritual. Preparation to relax, energize, open up to spirit, allow the energy, thoughts, and words to flow through me and connect me to the audience. Yes, the ritual is working. The breath is coming back. The angst of the blow to my gut subsides and I shelve the idea about whether or not I'm truly a "joyful woman" to deal with another time. Also, I make a mental note to change my introduction and remove those three words:"A joyful woman."

What is Joy, Anyway?

Four years have passed since that day and I've yet to return those three words to my bio or introduction. I have also yet to return them to my life—or have I? *What is joy, anyway?* I wonder, as I look at *Journey to Joy*, the title of our next anthology book. I approach the book shelf and pull out *The Merriam-Webster Dictionary*. (I know I could look it up online, but I love the feel of a book in my hands and the whishing sound it makes as I leaf through its pages...)

JOY (noun)

1a: the emotion evoked by well-being, success, or good fortune, or by the prospect of possessing what one desires: *DELIGHT*
1b: the expression or exhibition of such emotion: *GAIETY*
2: a state of happiness or felicity: *BLISS*
3: a source or cause of delight

Okay, this doesn't sound completely foreign to me...hmmm...maybe I am a joyful woman! When I think about it, though, I realize I feel these emotions intermittently throughout my waking hours on a normal day, but that they are fleeting...and the problem I have with calling myself a "joyful woman" is that I experience too many other emotions during those same waking hours. And these emotions are heavy, negative, and not as romantic as the delight, gaiety, and bliss that define the word "joy."

Like one year at Christmastime when I drove back from the Mohegan Sun casino in Connecticut as we all laughed and talked in the car. *Boom!* Suddenly brought to attention, I saw a huge deer run out of the small space between two oncoming cars. Before I could hit the brakes or turn the wheel it careened head-on into my left front bumper.

"Did you hit that car?" asked my rattled friend as I slammed on the brakes and maneuvered the car to the side of the road.

"No—oh my God! I think it was a deer!"

We jumped out of the car and, sure enough, there she lay. Already dead, thank God. Wobbly and weak from shock, I could barely walk or feel my legs. I knew I couldn't handle seeing her suffer. Another driver—a good Samaritan—stopped also. A veterinarian ready to provide care for, or medicate, the animal if necessary, she assured us that the impact had ended this beautiful creature's life immediately and that she'd experienced no suffering. Tears welled up in my eyes. I was relieved, but still upset.

The police arrived, inspected our car, and determined we could drive it. After filling out the paperwork they told us we could go. I heard some movement and turned around to look at the field on the other side of the road on our way back to the car. Two fawns had emerged from the tall grass. They stood there wide-eyed, and though I knew they were looking for their mother, their eyes rested on me.

My heart felt as though it would burst. Upon seeing my reaction, the veterinarian driver came over and reassured us they were old enough to make it on their own. Their mother had spent plenty of time with them teaching them how to find food, where to sleep, and how to be safe, she said. I remember thinking, *how ironic, since the mother is now lying dead on the side of the road...*

Still shaken when we arrived home, I fixed myself a 7&7 to take the edge off. I felt raw and numb, yet I also felt blessed. Blessed that the mother deer had died immediately and that she hadn't suffered tremendous pain; blessed that, of all the people on the road at that very moment, our good Samaritan was a veterinarian; blessed that no one was hurt and that my car was still intact and drivable; and blessed that the two baby deer would be okay and that they had each other as they ventured into a new world.

I was blessed again a month later when I received the check from the insurance company for damages. I didn't use it to fix the fender; instead I used it to pay my mortgage. Yes, blessings come in all shapes and sizes. As I look back over the years I count the many blessings bestowed upon me...

Blessings By Number

Blessing Number One: "I'm healthy and vibrant and strong. I'm sexy and happy and rich." The affirmation I'd said to myself in the bath four years ago is one that I've carried with me since and believe to be true. Okay, at least, it's *mostly* true...I feel blessed and grateful to have healed my physical body. I feel vibrant, especially when I'm doing what I love with people that I love. I feel strong and centered in the conviction I have for the path and partners I've chosen in my life. And every day, I have glimpses, and sometimes even really big chunks, of happiness and joy. Yes, I said it -*joy!*

Blessing Number Two: Our business allows my partner and me the freedom to live wherever we choose. We packed up our longtime residence of New Jersey one year ago and moved to sunny southwest Florida—and when I say sunny, I really mean it! I never realized how much joy (yes, I said the word again) a little bit of sunshine and warmth can bring into my days...

Blessing Number Three: Our business provides me the opportunity to meet many inspiring and amazing women, so many of whom have afforded me such great insights, as they've shared their passions and purposes with me. These eye-opening and life-changing experiences have brought me—dare I say it?—tremendous joy...

I know that to feel blessed, I have to surround myself with happy, nurturing people who lift me up, support me, and love and honor me.

Blessings Beyond Number Three: The list continues with more blessings than I can count—my mom, sisters, brothers, nieces, nephews, and in-laws are all healthy and living life on their terms. My incredible partner shares my dreams, really likes me, and loves me more than I can imagine...

I exercise great freedom and enjoy the simple pleasures of life—a walk on the beach, a soothing cup of coffee with the Sunday morning crossword puzzle, driving with the top down as the wind blows though my hair and so much more. Am I blessed? You betcha!

Blessings Versus Joy

Are blessings the same as joy? I think so. Merriam-Webster thinks so, too. They call blessings "a state conducive to happiness," much like their definition of joy which is "a state of happiness." And the loop continues as they define happiness as "a state of well-being and contentment: JOY."

As I look at my life I can truly say I am content most of the time, and have the feeling of well-being almost always. I am alive and flowing with the bounty of life—all of it! If you ask me today if I am a happy woman, I will answer emphatically "yes!" And from now on, if you ask if I'm a joyful woman, I will definitely own my joy!

ABOUT THE AUTHOR: Sue Urda, a.k.a. 'The Connections Expert', is an Author, Speaker, Inspirer and Co-Founder of Powerful You! Women's Network and Powerful You! Publishing. Sue is a two-time honoree on INC Magazine's list of the 500 Fastest-Growing Private Companies. Her award-winning book, *Powerful Intentions Everyday Gratitude* and her two Amazon bestselling books are designed to inspire women to tap the inner wisdom of their hearts, feel their personal power, and live each day through deliberate creation and intent. Sue shares her business, personal and spiritual experiences to fulfill her mission of connecting women to each other, their visions & themselves for personal success and freedom.

Sue Urda
Author, Speaker, Inspirer
www.powerfulyou.com
www.sueurda.com
info@powerfulyou.com

The Boy Who Spoke From Heaven

Lisa Hamilton

I sat at the end of the hospital bed holding my little boy's hand. He would have turned eighteen only a week later. Though not my biological son, I raised him and watched him grow from a chubby little boy to within days of becoming a man. To me, this was my little Brett, a gift that came into my life and changed it forever. I looked into his beautiful blue eyes, not blinking back, the same eyes that hours before were filled with so much love and laughter as he darted out to skateboard.

We were just leaving for a day hike in Mammoth, California, with Brett, his little brother Mitch, their father Rick, my daughter Allie, and me—a last minute vacation before school started. The boys took off for a quick ride on their skateboards down the hill, as I packed our remaining lunch items. They planned to meet us at the bottom of the hill.

Rick, Allie, and I were in the jeep, top rolled back, taking in the sunshine and breathing in the unmistakable smell of fresh pine trees. Life seemed suspended in that moment of carefree bliss, not a worry in the world, a perfect lazy summer day. Turning the corner, we saw the boys heading downhill, playing and carving out long fluid patterns as if surfing on the perfect wave.

Brett came down the hill first, crossed our path at the intersection and, turning back to wave didn't see the manhole in the street before him. Life stopped. Time froze. Each second became a freeze frame as I witnessed him fall with the helpless agony of not being able to do anything.

I slammed on the brakes, parked the car in the middle of the street, and jumped out. In a blur, I watched helplessly as his father held him in his arms and tried desperately to save him, while at the same time saying good-bye. Within the hour Brett was taken by medivac air ambulance to the Renown Medical Center in Reno, Nevada, and pronounced brain dead shortly after on September 5, 2011.

I once heard a story about a mother who lost her twin boys when they were taken from her instantly one day by death. She collapsed under the burden of her grief and sobbed through her tears "I don't see why God made me!"

"Dear," said her aunt, who tended to her and was wiser in the ways of the Lord, "you are not yet made. God is making you now."

It is in your darkest hour that God is making you.

Mine had just begun.

Reconciliation

Though the pronouncement was made, nothing in the natural realm supported it. Brett was hooked up to respirators and, though they superficially sustained his life, I could see beyond to his heart that I knew, somehow, was still beating on its own.

"Brett," I said, "I love you. I don't care what they are saying. I know you hear me. I can see it in your eyes. I can feel it in your heart. I know you're still alive. Please, Brett, wake up before it's too late."

As a parent, you cannot accept the pronouncement of death. It was only when the donor society came to the door that reality sunk in.

"We're here to talk to you both," they explained, and asked if we would step into the other room to discuss some details. "Ten months ago, Brett contacted us and chose to give his organs to others as a donor. But because he was not yet eighteen, we need your signatures."

They were asking the impossible!

"We can't do that," I said, "We cannot give away our boy—I cannot give away my boy—even to save another life! Please, you must leave..."

We sat in his room—room 109—for three days, holding his hand, talking to his spirit.

"Brett, are you still there?" we pleaded "Are you coming back? Please, they are coming to take you..."

Frantically, we contacted doctors, specialists—anyone and everyone—nationwide who had any experience in reviving the brain. At times there seemed to be glimmers of hope, but they only ended in defeat. Not ready to give up the fight, we checked into a nearby Ronald McDonald housing facility for parents of children in the hospital in critical condition, allowing us to stay with Brett as close to 24/7 as possible.

We were assigned room 109, the same number as Brett's hospital room. Brett's cell phone message indicator went off just as we received our room keys. His phone had been flooded with messages from loved ones who hoped he'd answer and dispel the rumors. As I picked it up and turned it over, I saw it was the 109th message received.

This was no mistake, nor was it a coincidence. Things like this don't just happen. I knew God was trying to tell me something.

"What does that number mean—what are you trying to say to me?" I implored God to send me a sign.

I woke up the next morning and continued to call specialists, hoping beyond all hope that someone would have an answer, or a cure.

"God, I am ready now," I prayed. "Please tell me, is Brett going to come back? Can you bring him back?'

The numbers separated in my mind. I saw a ten, followed by a nine. I knew that numbers have significant spiritual meanings, and understood that God wanted to speak to me through these numbers. I spent the next hours researching to find everything I could about the meaning of these two numbers.

The number ten means the perfect end of a cycle—wanting nothing, complete.

The number nine means an ending with a perfect movement forward. My research found that Christ died on the ninth hour, and that through his death he brought others life.

Finally, I was reconciled. Brett's life was an end to a perfect cycle. Yet, there would be a perfect movement forward; his death would also bring life to others. Not just physical life, but spiritual life as well. His life would encapsulate all those around him, and Brett's spirit would remain.

"Thank you, God," my heart whispered. The fight was over, but I didn't feel defeated.

I felt like the hand of God was upon me as He said "follow me through the shadow of death, but fear no evil. Death is but a shadow. There is life that goes on forever."

Sacrifice Of Love

That day we went into Brett's room not to talk to him but to talk with him.

"Brett," we said as we held his hand and looked into his eyes, more crystal blue than ever before. "We know you're still alive, though not in this body anymore. We aren't here to say good-bye, because we don't have to. Help us to always feel you, and sense your presence. Though you may be in heaven with God, we still need you in our lives. Give us signs. Give us a message. Never stop letting us know that you are alive."

We had one last request: "Brett, give us courage to fulfill your desire. Help us to release you into the lives of others."

It was in this darkest hour that God was making Brett's father and me, and I understood the depth of love God has for the world. In giving His son so that we could be saved, He illustrated a love that sacrifices—at all costs—to save another.

Rather than wait, we initiated the phone call to say we were ready to sign. I felt Brett's presence right there beside me, as if he was in the room approving our signatures on the necessary documents.

"Please," I asked, "tell me whose lives will be saved?"

I listened and heard the stories of other children fighting for their lives, like Brett, in hospital rooms like his, this very night. Their chances of survival, to receive a transplant match in time, were one in a thousand and dawn would most likely come as the last good-byes were spoken.

I knew the pain of a mother's heart, and the desperate prayers in the midnight hour that pleaded for a miracle. I felt Brett's spirit between us, as if he was grabbing our hands to his heart, and asking us "will you help me save them? They need me now, are you ready?"

"Yes," my heart answered. "We're ready."

We returned to room 109 to say good-bye. Yet this time there was no shadow of death, no fear. This time I knew beyond a shadow of a doubt that Brett could hear and see me.

"Do you know I love you?" I asked him as I looked straight into his eyes. I saw the love still in his eyes and knew he was saying "yes."

The doctors came to log the surgery time on the board. It was 10:09 p.m. on 9/10/2011. The tenth hour, the ninth month, Brett's life was a perfect cycle and a perfect moving forward, as he courageously went to save the lives of others. I felt honored to have been chosen to witness the highest act of love imaginable.

The hours passed as we waited in the room. Suddenly we awakened to the sound of helicopters. I glanced at the clock. It was 5:59 a.m.

"Yes, Brett, I know—ten nine...now go," I assured him. "Do what you had planned ten months ago. Hurry before it's too late. I am proud of you, son. Prouder than I have ever been."

Though I'd never meet the mothers whose children were saved that night, in spirit we shared the same joy—celebrated the same victory that by-passed even death—and I was privileged to be part of the miracle.

The helicopters left as quickly as they came, due to the urgency of their cargo. In that moment, seeing the helicopters fade away in the distance, I felt as if God, Brett, Rick, and I were standing there all together, experiencing the profound magnitude of answered prayer, not only from a mother kneeling by a bedside, but my own prayer of courage.

Brett's celebration of life ceremony started the beginning of a movement: Room 109. I passed out 109 T-shirts that day, with a majestic heavenly griffin holding a banner that said "Life" and inscribed:

Give it up...There's more...Room 109

I reflected upon the past weeks—seemingly a lifetime ago—and heard the voice of God say: "Look up that scripture."

"What scripture?" I thought, "there is none on the T-shirt..." Bewildered, I continued to stare. And then I saw it: Romans 10:9.

"If you believe in your heart that God brought Christ back from the dead, you will be saved."

"Yes," I confessed, I believe. Now it's up to me to continue to have faith in God with the same courage as my boy who spoke to me from heaven.

ABOUT THE AUTHOR: Founder of V.I.N.E. FOUNDATION Lisa Hamilton is dedicated to her passion and mission to rescue distressed women in financial and emotional crisis, and to help them transform broken lives into new beginnings. Lisa's candidly honest and humorous book *Unstick your Stuck Life* is an accumulation of her expertise with helping others discover their life purpose and true core essence, drawing from deep spiritual insight. Overcoming her own life crisis, Lisa is a freelance writer for the Los Angeles Times newspaper, and a respected speaker. She lives in Laguna Beach as well as the mountains of Mammoth Lakes, California with her daughter Allie.

Lisa Hamilton
Founder V.I.N.E. FOUNDATION
www.lisahamilton.com
vinefoundation@mac.com

PART TWO

The Blessings of Relationship

*"So, relationship is one of the
most powerful tools for growth...
If we look honestly at our relationships,
we can see so much about how we have created them."
~ Shakti Gwain*

Loss, Truth, and Love
Donna Visco

I fumbled outside the door for my keys as I arrived home after a day of picnicking with good friends. My daughter was out and I looked forward to a quiet restful evening. I finally opened the door and our orange cat Guido bolted out of the house, something he'd never done before.

Why's he acting so weird? I thought as I grabbed him, knowing he didn't like to venture outside. It was then I heard the house phone ringing, and ran to answer it.

"Donna, you have to get to Elizabeth General Hospital—Joe's had a heart attack!" my friend's alarmed voice informed me. I froze.

Joe, my husband of twenty-four years, passed away before I arrived at the hospital. My mind reeled as my brain screamed, *How could he die? He's fit! He passed his stress test a year ago, no problem. Why now—when our relationship is at such a low point?*

Separated for the prior three months, our marriage had been hurting for a long time. I remembered the day a year before when my office phone rang and it was Joe, so upset he was crying. Frightened—I'd never heard him like this—I listened as he tearfully informed me that his position as a lieutenant in the police department was in jeopardy.

He revealed he had a longtime girlfriend who'd put in place a restraining order against him. In that instant, I envisioned my marriage as a major car crash, a horrible accident at an intersection with bodies that appeared badly injured, bloodied, and broken. I felt crushed on every level. Still, I could tell Joe was scared, sorry, and ashamed, and knew I had to be strong for my family.

This new truth made things clear to me instantly. After an attempt at counseling, we ultimately decided we couldn't make it as a couple. Joe was clear: He didn't love me and had no desire to make our marriage work, although he wanted to keep the framework of our loveless marriage in place for the sake of our children. I came to accept his terms and felt I had no choice.

My emotional life had gaping holes—major loss, major pain—and all I could do was maintain being a mother to my two children and live my life as best I could. When I decided Joe and I couldn't live together anymore and that we needed to separate, I hoped on some level he would miss me and realize he did love me after all.

One night, about a month after we separated, I called Joe to see if it would be cool if I visited him. I felt particularly lonely and missed him in spite of all the pain. While there, I suggested I might stay the night—I thought perhaps we could be together, not necessarily sexually, but to support each other on some level.

When he said no, I was devastated. I left and cried all the way home. Way too painful, I knew I could no longer do this to myself. I had to accept the truth and told myself: *He doesn't love you Donna, you must move on—enough!*

I believe he loved me as a person, but no longer as a wife, and I know now he was protecting me that night from myself and my false hope that we might have had a future as a couple.

Is That All There Is?

In addition to losing Joe, I'd lost several family members unexpectedly within the ten years leading up to his death. My mother and father had passed at the ages of fifty-eight and fifty-nine, respectively, and my forty-year-old sister and thirty-seven-year-old brother had died young as well. Where were all these people, these precious souls I loved, who'd passed away? How can you love someone, they die and *that's it?* I knew there had to be more to life than what I had experienced. I needed answers!

I desperately wanted to understand more and at a deeper level. If there was a heaven I surely didn't want to wait until I got there to know more about it! I prayed, but never felt confident of understanding or achieving peace in my life. There was always a gnawing knot in my solar plexus that felt as normal as breathing. It was that natural.

I began my search for good teachers: Anthony Robbins, Deepak Chopra, and Master Choa Kok Sui helped me make the greatest shifts in consciousness. In the earliest years of my waking up, I attended many of Anthony Robbins' programs and scraped off the veneer of old belief systems ("BS"), which made it easier for me to open up to new ideas.

Boy, did I have a lot of "BS" that caused major issues in my life! A lot of internal dialogue reinforced that I was stuck because I wasn't good enough, smart enough, or strong enough. Afraid to move in a new direction and be wrong, I carried within me a great deal of pain. Through a series of exercises and self-work, I began to see how these belief systems prevented me from living my life fully.

For example, I'd held onto the idea that *I will never have someone who'll love me for who I am, just as I am,* and believed that Joe might love me again like he did years ago as long as I hung in there. Deep down I couldn't understand why I was unable to regain his love. In retrospect, Joe had held onto the belief that as long as he had the framework of his family, despite the weakness of our relationship, everything would be okay. *Were we wrong!* I started to take a good look at what stood between me and the life I desired.

My next great teacher was Deepak Chopra, who taught me I was on a journey to find myself—a journey to my soul. Through meditation—a profound shift for me—I began to understand my life had purpose; I could design and create the life I desired and manifest *anything*—both good and bad.

I discovered the happy soft gentle soul within, and began to take stock. The more conscious a thinker I became, the more gratitude filled the spaces in my life and I found so much to feel joyful about. I had two beautiful children, wonderful friends, a healthy body, and a strong desire to do something in this lifetime. I just didn't know exactly what that was yet.

Enter my next great teacher, Master Choa Kok Sui, whose Pranic Healing changed my life completely. I knew I was a soul in a body having a human experience, but what was I here to do? Then I learned I was here to heal.

Heal? Yes, heal! The energy that animates my body, moves my arms, allows me to see, hear, feel, taste, and smell, and fills me with love, peace, and joy is who I *am*. Hmmm...and I can use this energy and my connection to God to help others who have a veneer so thick they can't see they are amazing souls looking to find their way in this experience...

Little by little, I learned that I am the creator and the producer of my life. There had been so many signs along the way beckoning me to pay attention, that something was wrong, yet I put blinders up to avoid the painful truth. Like Joe's lack of attention and unreasonable anger—I'd think, *he's not in a good mood today,* and rationalize so as not to experience pain.

I couldn't go back and re-orchestrate my life; the best I could do was look back and learn. There were some expensive lessons in my past and I needed to make the most of them. Like learning to pay attention to the moment and how it affects my life.

How to Manifest My Own Destiny

How could I move forward to create the life I desired? I wanted to know! Gradually, I began to see that gaining consciousness really was a life-long journey and that I always had, and have, a *choice*. I control from within how I want to design my life—consciously or unconsciously.

I believe the joy I experience today comes from creating my life *every day*. Conscious of the seeds I plant, I enjoy the harvest of good planting from earlier days. Most importantly, I believe I'm living my life's purpose through the work I do. I feel on purpose and joyful leading yoga, meditations, teaching, and healing.

About a year and a half after Joe passed away, as I shifted my world view and created the intention of a new and better life, I met Rick—a good man with a good heart. I better respected myself and gained faith that I deserved happiness and a good life. I started to make sure I took in the beauty of everyday life, some way, somehow, whether it was a soft couch and a good book, the sun shining through my window, or my granddaughter kissing my cheek.

Today, only good things come to mind when I think of Joe. I remember he was a good friend, and I cherish the moments of tenderness and caring we shared. He was also an excellent father, and I'm grateful for our time together with our two amazing children, who created the wonderful grandchildren he would have adored.

I am at a place of peace that goes deep. The gnawing feeling in my stomach is long gone, now replaced with a feeling of warmth—a gradual shift that didn't happen overnight. Imagine walking a path with sparse vegetation and watching that vegetation slowly change and grow more abundant and lush. Before you know it, you're in a beautiful place surrounded by people you love, who love you! You remember your path and realize it was the choices you made along your journey that got you there.

I'm not sure who first said "you are a soul having a human experience," but I am forever grateful for those words. Eventually it became clear that I was *not* Donna, a mother, sister, friend, teacher, or lover. Those were merely roles my soul was playing. Now I understand I am a soul having a human experience and I make the choices that create my life!

I feel God has been very generous to me, and that my ability to teach and heal affords me opportunities to share with others what I have learned. I inhale, embrace, revere, and savor every moment, as I am grateful that life—including loss, truth, and love—is *this soul's* gift!

ABOUT THE AUTHOR: Donna's core message is love yourself, relax and have fun! She shares extensive knowledge of Body, Mind and Spirit through the Science of Pranic Healing and teaching Deepak Chopra's Meditation, Perfect Health and Yoga courses since 2002. As a Pranic Healer working with life force energy, Donna has a private practice and is a Teacher of Level One and Advanced Pranic Healing at the College of St Elizabeth and Hospital venues. Donna's passion is to assist others to love themselves, find inner peace and understand the gift that they are and the gift that life is! Her passion is sharing this message!

Donna Visco
Pranic Healing and Meditation Teacher
www.pranichealingatblcssedland.com
serdonna@aol.com
908-688-7974

Imperfectly Perfect

Sheila Turner

I *don't* do daily affirmations, I *do* get super stressed out sometimes—I forget my kids' orthodontist appointments, can't remember what I had for lunch—and have crowned myself "mother of the year" for all the wrong reasons more times than I can count.

I'd like to tell you my life has been filled with joy beyond measure, but it hasn't. I'd like to say my journey to joy has been an easy one, but I can't. Not too many people will tell you that joy comes from knowing and accepting that life happens, plans change, traffic sucks, grocery lines are long, and dinner rolls burn way too quickly—but I will.

You won't see *my* joy on my face or view it in my step. It's not a joy I shout from the rooftops; it's completely internal—a joy I experience every single day in the middle of my crazy, forgetful, stressful, busy life.

In fact, I struggled with writing about joy for a long time because my perceived notion of a "joyful" person was not *me*. You see, I'm a realist. My feet are planted firmly on the ground. It wasn't until I realized that *my* journey to joy consists *not* of arriving at complete peace, but of continuing to do what I do while appreciating the blessings in each and every day. I had to let go of the thought that in order to qualify, I had to be "joyful" on the outside, too. And as backwards as it sounds, *my* joy comes from being comfortable with my "imperfect self" and my "imperfect world."

I don't need my house to be spotless, Christmas isn't ruined if I don't get everything on the kids' lists, and I'm ok with cereal for dinner because I didn't have time to get to the grocery store. And the extra five pounds I can't seem to lose? Well, I'm not going to let that, or the rest of those little things, ruin my day, my week, my month, my year, or my life.

I like the fact that I don't let the little things consume me. I see so many women who want everything perfect all of the time. Such intense stress and pressure creates a world focused too much on "things" and not enough on "meanings." The pursuit of perfection—or emphasis on a final outcome—can blind one to the memories and meaningful moments that happen continuously. I am thankful every single day that I have the ability to appreciate the process, rather than insist on a perfect outcome.

I learned that lesson the hard way when I was twenty-two years old, married only seven weeks, and my husband was diagnosed with brain cancer. Needless to say, the typical newlywed quarrels about leaving the toilet seat up or the cap off the toothpaste tube suddenly became incredibly insignificant. I knew those things weren't worth fighting over—what I *didn't* know was that gaining that perspective marked the beginning of my journey.

The Imperfections

Kyle and Eve lost their dad to cancer when they were just ten and six years old, respectively. Before that they watched him endure seizures, MRIs, surgeries, radiation, and chemotherapy, and never had the chance to live in a safe, stable world. As their mother, I dreaded the day I'd have to tell them it was time to say goodbye.

What I failed to see then was that *their* journey started the day they were born into this imperfect world. Just like me, they lived their lives every day knowing that leaving the cap off the toothpaste tube, or getting stuck in traffic and arriving ten minutes late for a birthday party wasn't going to ruin their day, week, month, year, or their lives.

The imperfection of their childhood led them to become the most compassionate, thoughtful, appreciative, and thankful children I know. They look at this world differently because they know life isn't to be taken for granted. They have this sense, this *perspective*—far beyond their years—that could have destroyed them, but taught them instead to appreciate the journey along the way, and not to focus on a perfect outcome...

I honestly didn't know if I'd ever see them smile again after their dad's passing. It's been more than three years now and their joy is stronger than ever! To see them smile, hear them laugh—or even tell a corny joke—gives me a joy I cannot begin to describe. To watch them love life again is my proudest accomplishment, because it could have gone a very different way...

They often remember their dad through pictures and stories, but most importantly, they choose to celebrate their dad and his life by helping other kids who've lost loved ones as well. A few months after their father passed I sent Kyle and Eve to Camp Erin, a free bereavement camp for kids who've lost a loved one. Their grief counselor told me being around other kids who've suffered a loss like theirs could make an unbelievable difference in their lives. While I wasn't crazy about letting them out of my sight for an entire weekend, I trusted her, sent them, and am eternally indebted to the foundation, staff, and volunteers who changed our lives forever.

Since that weekend, Kyle and Eve have been asked on numerous occasions to write and speak about their journey and their commitment to living life to its fullest. They begged me to send them to Camp Erin for a second year so they could help the "new kids" feel comfortable and welcome. And they did just that! When I picked them up after that weekend, counselors overwhelmed me with story after story about how my children took the time to talk to, comfort, and show new campers they were not alone in their grief.

Our mission to spread the word and share our story went national in the fall of 2011. While on the set of Anderson Cooper's talk show about surviving grief, Anderson asked Kyle if he cries much. Without hesitation Kyle replied "I do cry a lot, but what I know is that it's ok to cry. Crying helps you—you are not weak, you are strong."

Anderson, who lost his father when he was only ten years old, told Kyle he was absolutely right—crying is a sign of strength. Our message on the show that day resonated with so many viewers that the producer called me the next day to say he'd never seen so much positive feedback from any of their previous shows!

The Detour

After the death of my husband, I knew I'd be fine raising Kyle and Eve alone, and got comfortable with the idea of being the quintessential single mom. I was settling into this new life when along came a major detour I didn't see coming. Oh, I was used to detours and changes in plans for sure, but not quite ready for one of this magnitude!

Did I mention that this detour has a name? Yes, his name is Jeff. Jeff was someone I knew casually through mutual friends who happened to live down the street. He traveled for work and was barely ever home. When he was, he'd wave as I drove by. I didn't know very much about him, just that I'd heard he was a great guy.

A relationship was the last thing I thought about. The kids and I had been through so much—the thought of getting out into the dating world made me uncomfortable. Of course, at only thirty-seven years old, I knew at some point friends would try to set me up and get me out there again. But not this soon, I thought...

How much time do I give myself? I wondered. *Will I wake up one morning and say today's the day I'm ready to do this? Will I have an aha! moment, or listen to other people who are more than happy to give me their opinions?* I couldn't believe how many friends, acquaintances, and even strangers were willing to chime in on the topic. I got a lot of "you should do this" and "you should do that," "give yourself at least a year," and—well, you get the picture...

As you probably guessed, it happened sooner than I'd planned. My next door neighbor knew Jeff's family well and, as time went by, I caught on to her little mission to get us together. So I took a chance and went on a date with him. My life—until then a rollercoaster full of twists, turns, loops, and heart-dropping moments—had given me the courage to listen to my heart and find out where this detour would take me. And boy was I in for quite a ride!

The first day of summer, a little over a year after our first date, I found myself standing at the top of a gorgeous grand staircase in Hawaii as beautiful Eve—my maid of honor—held my hand. In the gazebo below stood Jeff with handsome Kyle as his best man, waiting for us to join them and begin our new lives together. It was just the four of us in the most beautiful and peaceful place on earth, celebrating an amazing moment on our journey.

This is also where the kids gave Jeff his new name—Kepi. It's his Hawaiian name and will forever be a reminder of that moment in time where we tossed all the worries of the world aside and simply enjoyed our days as a family.

I think back to that time right before our first date, and realize that had I restricted myself to a timeframe and listened to those who said it was too soon, I would have missed out. A really great man who brings such happiness to me and my kids every single day, Jeff make us laugh, love, and enjoy life. He respects Kyle and Eve's need to remember their dad, and is incredibly supportive of our efforts to help others who've lost loved ones. He loves us, works hard for us, and shows us every single day that we are his number one priority. I couldn't imagine not having him in our lives and sharing in our journey.

My Joy, My Job...

My joy is simple—but not always easy. It lies in knowing that this life, world, and universe encompass so much more than me. There will always be twists and turns— good twists and bad twists, great turns and not-so-great turns—that will be out of my control, and missed appointments, traffic jams, sadness and sorrow, burnt dinner rolls, and long lines at the grocery store. Those are guarantees.

My job is not to let these things swallow up my joy. *My* job is to do all I can to recognize that joy shines through the clouds every single day of this beautiful gift we call life...

ABOUT THE AUTHOR: Sheila Turner is a business owner, realtor, speaker, supporter of cancer and grief organizations, a wife and mother of 2 children. She studied Speech Communications and Public Relations, speaks on behalf of The Moyer Foundation, appeared on "The Anderson (Cooper) Show", and writes an online forum for parents of grieving children called "CampErinParents.com". Sheila has been published in, *Women Living Consciously*, and featured by Penn Wissahickon Hospice, The Philadelphia Tribune, WHYY Radio and the Leukemia and Lymphoma Society. Her newest venture is F.A.B. Women Fitness combining workouts with personal development – A workout that's as essential as your little black dress!

Sheila Turner
www.fromthetopdance.com
www.fab-women.com
info@sheilaturner.com
610-613-0322

Thrive & Shine
Through Sorrow
Mary Rives, MS, CPC

I was sitting on our New England porch with my dear friend Annie, a gifted psychotherapist, when I got the call. The news was too unfathomable to absorb.

"No! It can't be Woody!" I insisted as I handed the phone to Annie. Robert "Woody" Woodward, our dearest family friend (and honorary uncle to our son Rene), allegedly was wrongfully shot by police, and died a slow, agonizing death without any loved ones by his side. I made a beeline for the freezer that held an emergency cigarette sealed in a glass jar. Unable to open the jar, I grabbed a hammer and shattered the glass. I ran outside and, collapsing under a pine tree, inhaled the soothing smoke deep into my lungs.

I later discovered that my reaction to such shocking news paled in comparison to our eighteen year-old son's, who cried out in agony as his body crumpled to the floor at the foot of the stairs. Telling Rene that "our Woody" was dead proved to be the most difficult thing my husband Keith and I have ever done. We held him in our arms, weeping as one.

The Way We Were...

I'll always remember the first time I saw Woody. A single mother in my mid-twenties in Washington, D.C., I was relieved to have a rare weekend off from parenting thanks to my folks, who took three-year-old Rene for the weekend. I loved Halloween and the chance to express myself creatively, and that year I dressed up as a feral cat and headed to a party at a cooperative house referred to as "Club Wayne."

Situated near the health food cooperative in Takoma Park, where I worked at that time as a collective member during my return to college, Club Wayne had similarities to the spacious group house of peace activists where I resided in the heart of D.C. But Club Wayne was comprised of nerdy astronomers and this enigmatic character named Woody.

He sat in a circle with the others, his handsome face—reminiscent of a young Robert Redford—illuminated by candlelight, the music of Talking Heads in the background. He cast his warm gaze upon me, and his sky blue eyes locked with mine for a moment I'm grateful to remember so vividly now. Surprised to feel sparks with this good-looking guy, I stood transfixed as he regaled the group with a story about hiking in the Sierra Nevadas. His soft, mellow voice and whimsical laugh captured my heart immediately.

Our first date was an autumnal walk during which we spoke about the things that mattered to us—intentional community, vegetarianism, social justice, and children.

It soon became apparent that the spark between us was mutual. Woody told me he'd be leaving for New England within six months, returning to his roots where he'd be free to live closer to nature, work with troubled teenagers, and care for his grandparents, whose ancestors came to America on the Mayflower.

"You can take the boy out of New England, but you can't take New England out of the boy," he told me with a sheepish grin.

When I saw how wonderful he was with Rene, I told him I was game for six months of fun-loving intimacy—how could I not be, when the joy experienced by the three of us was so magical! Unbeknownst to me, this decision would change my life—and Rene's—in ways we couldn't begin to imagine.

As the end of a delightful six months came to its expected close, a drunken Woody tearfully poured out his deeper feelings for me one night —obviously he'd become more attached to me and Rene than he'd bargained for. Since there was now a strong bond between him and Rene, we agreed to nurture our friendship from afar.

A year later, Woody met up with us at the Rainbow Gathering in Vermont where I met my future husband, Keith. We were sitting around the same campfire and, in typical Woody fashion (and a portent of his future place within our family) he hoisted Rene onto his shoulders and took off for an adventure, leaving me time to better get to know Keith.

Instead of being the best man at our hippie wedding on a communal farm in Maryland, Woody was "best fool!" He allowed the children to remove his clothes down to his boxers and paint his body with bright and beautiful colors. We clapped a happy rhythm as our colorful clown danced barefoot, children giggling at his side. From that day forward, Woody's place in our family firmament was assured.

Despite being my former lover, Woody quickly became Keith's best friend—they shared a mutual love of music and art. In addition, Woody took on the role of unofficial parenting advisor and advocate for my young Rene.

Woody honored his deeper nature, and always had the courage to follow his heart. He'd slow us down from the bustle of modern life, and kindly gave generously of his time. He loved playing family games like charades and shooting hoops with Rene. They'd take our dogs for long walks in the forest and be gone for hours, returning muddy and grinning from ear to ear.

The Pied Piper's Family

Once married, we relocated to Massachusetts where Woody became a regular visitor. Our proximity to his beloved New England haunts meant that Woody figured prominently in our lives, and his friendship with Keith flourished through their frequent contact. The bonds deepened, as did our interdependence and love.

Woody's anti-establishment lifestyle sometimes made him critical of our middle-class luxuries, yet he readily took advantage of the amenities we enjoyed. Often he'd show up for supper—he had a finely tuned "dinner radar"—just as we were sitting down to eat. We always welcomed him, knowing he would "earn his keep" by doing chores and helping with homework. His knack for befriending families with children led him to become an unofficial big brother, uncle, or mentor figure easily. A playmate and teacher, Woody played the "Pied Piper" to kids, dogs, and parents alike.

He'd figured prominently in our family's long-term plans until his death that fateful day in 2001 when it all came crashing down around us. We realized that ultimately we had no choice but to move on without him. Buried with him were our mutual dreams of co-creating a retirement center for expatriates in a developing country, or even simply having a guest cottage where Woody could hang his hat when he came to town.

Immersed in grief, I found it difficult to function in a world that was oblivious to my family's overwhelming sorrow, and I reeled from the challenges inherent in the strange new quiet of a home bereft of Woody's presence. I made the painful decision to let go of my fulfilling job as director of a local family center because of my intensely vacillating emotions and a newfound inability to focus on work. Amidst the trauma, it was nothing short of a miracle that I completed graduate school, an undertaking that Woody had fully supported.

Sometimes I'd swing from intense anger into profound sorrow. I listened to music Woody loved, tears streaming down my face, and find myself in denial, pretending he was on one of his adventures and would walk through the door at any moment. How could these joyous homecomings be over forever? Helpless to change the mourning we needed to experience as a family, I realized that we could seek justice in Woody's name.

For two exhausting years we spent many freezing mornings on street corners in the New England town where Woody was killed, holding signs of protest while making our voices heard. Several local strangers offered their support and quickly became cherished friends. After some semblance of justice was accomplished and Woody's family settled out of court, we resigned from our efforts— satisfied that measures were adopted to ensure a similar senseless tragedy never happens again.

Laughter *Is* The Best Medicine...

By this time my once stable family exhibited classic symptoms of Post Traumatic Stress Disorder (PTSD). In our gloomy isolation, the realization struck that the best way to honor Woody was not by sinking further into despair, but by simplifying our lives, lightening up, and living in ways that would reflect his beautiful spirit.

I recognized it was high time to take action to help bring joy into our lives again. I discovered Laughter Yoga, and I practically leapt at the opportunity to train with Dr. Madan Kataria, co-founder of the Laughter Yoga movement.

While it took some cajoling to rouse Keith from his torpor, we were absolutely delighted to be absurdly laughing for no reason among kindred spirits. We used the practice of laughter to actively incorporate joy into our lives while simultaneously offering the gift of Laughter Yoga to others. It proved to be an effective mind/body method for shifting our energy while simultaneously honoring the memory of our delightful friend.

After our son married and began a new life with his lovely wife, our empty nest invited us to formulate a clear vision for our lives. We sold our home, hit the open road in an RV, and initiated the manifestation of our long-held dream of traveling to find a fulfilling new life within the oasis of intentional community...

"There's Nothing That The Road Cannot Heal."
~ Conor Oberst

The waves of grief slowly subsided as the miles passed beneath our wheels. Our freshly minted laughter practice enabled us to embrace challenging moments with the conscious and powerful use of levity. At times, our post-traumatic stress attempted to resurface, challenging us to keep our heads above emotional waters. However, our determination to thrive in spite of our adversity would not be deterred. Tears came and went, but PTSD was no match for our mutual goal of renewed joyful living.

After traveling ten thousand miles, through twenty-three states and thirty-one communities, we settled in sunny New Mexico and now reside in an eco-conscious cohousing community in Santa Fe. There we foster friendships, create meaningful work, and enjoy living the life of our dreams.

Our recovery from Woody's loss stands as a testament to the healing power of love and laughter, as well as to the ability of grief to be used as a transformational tool. Although we'd give anything to have him back, Woody's spirit lives on. His goodness is embodied in our hearts and in the joy that we share in his honor. We've learned that people *can* recover, heal, and transform their lives—even in the face of great odds—and now are deeply committed to helping coach others to create bright, beautiful, and joy-filled lives. Through our *Thrive and Shine Coaching* services, we utilize unique techniques—including laughter—to assist professional performers and serenity-seeking baby boomers to thrive and shine through life's sorrows and joys...

ABOUT THE AUTHOR: As a Coach, Mary empowers performers to shine on stage and thrive in life. Mary first earned her PhD at "The School of Hard Knocks", followed by her Master of Science degree at Antioch University. Certified as a Laughter Yoga Leader by Dr. Madan Kataria, a former actor and the founder of Laughter Yoga International, she became certified as a Professional Life and Laughter Coach by The Levity Institute. Mary happily resides in Santa Fe, New Mexico, a thriving hub of the television and film industries. One of her greatest joys is helping others experience wild success with their creative expression and endeavors.

Mary Rives, MS, CPC
Thrive and Shine Coaching of Laughter Inc, LLC
www.ThriveandShine.com
mary@ThriveandShine.com
505-954-1350

Independence Day
Charlotte Beilgard

"Say another word and I'll slit your throat!" L.J. threatened. He grabbed the phone on which I was talking to Melissa and hung it up. Terror-stricken, my heart pounded, my hands trembled, and my mind raced. *Oh my God!* I thought, *my husband thinks I'm plotting to leave him!*

"I should cut out your heart and see if it's made of wood!" he snarled and ordered me to sit on the sofa across from his chair in our living room. "And don't try to call the police, because if they come I'll stab you in the heart before they can get in to save you!"

I closed my eyes in desperation and asked God to do for me what I could not do for myself—I told him that if I got out of that apartment alive, it would never happen again; my life was going to change. I hoped and prayed that it wasn't too late...

The Beginning

Born to older parents, I was the youngest of four children. Unplanned, my mother told me how she cried when she found out she was pregnant with me—how could they afford another child? In her late thirties, my mother's health was never again the same. I felt in the pit of my stomach I was a mistake—responsible for my mother's pain and suffering, so I grew up trying to make her happy.

My mother and father—adult children of alcoholic parents—became very religious and taught me from birth to fear God. I'd surely be sent to hell if I wasn't a perfect little Christian! So, I became "Little Miss Perfect" to please any and all authority figures. I was told to "die out to the flesh," which I thought meant to shut down my feelings and become numb.

Only allowed to be with kids of the same religion, at fifteen I was told to date only boys of the same faith. I met my ex-husband at a nearby church's youth rally. L.J. was possessive, controlling, and jealous when I was with my other friends—he wanted to keep me all to himself—and I mistook that for love. It felt right because it was so familiar, just like my home and church life.

By seventeen we were engaged. Married the June before my eighteenth birthday, I was determined to make him happy. After all, I'd learned how to please my parents, my teachers, my pastor, and all the other authority figures, of course I could please him too!

However, his wants changed every day. The first few years of marriage I struggled to please him, but couldn't seem to get it right. He'd backhand me occasionally if I did something to upset him, and was verbally, sexually, and emotionally abusive. At the time, I didn't see it as abusive—I thought it was his God-given right because he was my husband. I remember thinking he'd never really hurt me because he loved me, so I never told anyone.

Two years later I gave birth to our son, Scott, and three years later to our daughter, Melissa. A wonderful father when they were very young, L.J. gave the children lots of love and attention. The story changed as they grew into teenagers. Scott could never please his father and L.J. physically abused him. Scott had an attention deficit challenge, and in his father's eyes was not the "perfect" son.

Living with his physically, verbally, and emotionally abusive father was like living in a pressure cooker. Melissa, on the other hand, witnessed the abuse. When her father came home, she'd hide in her room and read books. A very quiet child, she stopped eating almost completely at seventeen.

I worked two jobs and didn't realize what was going on for a while. Melissa lost her will to live if it meant growing up to be like *me*, her mother! Distraught, I determined to find help for her; I couldn't let her die! I placed her in a treatment center for eating disorders to save her life—but it turned out to be the beginning of saving mine...

Co-Dependent No More!

They counseled us as a family during the six weeks she was in treatment. That's when I realized I was co-dependent (I was born that way, I believe), and that I needed to take back my life, quit taking care of everyone else, and stop pleasing others in order to feel I was good enough and not a mistake.

L.J. refused to attend any of the sessions—after all, it was *our* problem, not his. Depressed and hopeless about our marriage, I realized I was on a sinking ship and had two choices—get off or go down with it. Although I was afraid of going to hell if I divorced him, I realized I was already living in hell and dying a slow death. I decided I needed to divorce him, and that was when I emotionally left the marriage.

Once he felt my energy shift he became like a tiger in a cage. He told me to "watch my back." I started to plan my escape with a knot in my stomach.

I worked as an apartment manager, and we lived on the property. That Saturday I was off from work, and when Melissa called to see if I wanted to go to the mall with her, he thought we were talking about me leaving him! That's when he pulled the knife!

I sat on the sofa and prayed for God to intervene, and our telephone rang. It was the apartment answering service, and the lady explained that the maintenance man on call didn't answer. There was an emergency, and an elderly resident was hysterical because her toilet was overflowing.

Ok, I thought with a heavy heart, *I've got to think fast!*

"L.J., I've *got* to check it out—it's old Mrs. Henderson! You know, the woman who can barely see?"

"Ok," he growled, "but I'm going with you!"

I knew that if I could just get outside the apartment I had a chance of staying alive. We walked down the sidewalk toward the office together. I looked down the street ahead of us and saw the security guard on one side of the street, and then spotted a policeman on the other. I didn't know it then, but my son-in-law had called the police when my daughter told him what she'd heard over the phone.

Hallelujah! Overcome with relief, I dropped to my knees to thank God as L.J. ran for cover into the office to hide the knife. My nightmare was over! And so was my twenty-five year marriage. Heartbroken, I sobbed, when suddenly I heard a voice whisper in my ear: "God can mend a broken heart, if you'll give him all the pieces." And that was my new beginning...

Celebrating Me!

And so began my journey to joy. I started attending CoDA meetings, a 12-Step fellowship program of men and women whose common purpose is to develop healthy relationships. I knew I had to develop a healthy relationship with myself as well as with others, and I dug down deep to excavate my true self—the one that had gotten lost in people pleasing. I worked hard to find out how and why I became a person without needs and wants, and why I'd settled for such a shell of a life. I learned how to let go of my limiting beliefs, extreme fear of God and authority figures, and take back my power.

I wrote poetry and celebrated the precious little girl who believed she was a mistake, and who tried not to rock the boat and disappoint others. I began to trust my inner voice and believe in myself, as I embraced my true worth. In time, I was able to forgive my ex-husband, my parents, the church, and myself.

I know they all loved me in their own way, but I didn't love myself. Today I am so thankful for the wonderful gifts I've been given, especially since I escaped such a near-tragedy and what I thought at the time was the end of my world. Little did I know then, it was only the beginning...

As an inspirational speaker, spiritual mentor, a Certified Passion Test Facilitator, and a Certified Dream Builder Coach, I love being on stage, playing big, and feel such joy as I facilitate workshops, seminars, and talks around the world.

I write poetry and publish an inspirational newsletter to empower women to embrace their magnificence, believe in themselves, share their gifts and talents, and show up in the world in all of their greatness! As they discover, recover, and celebrate their God-given gifts and talents and step into their greatness, they create juicy, prosperous, passionate, and joyful lives, and live their life's purpose *on purpose!*

As I help to empower others, I am reminded daily of the *old* me—the person I was before I loved and respected myself and my own needs. The joy of helping others honor their own light, respect their own true natures, and learn to revel in their unique creative capability fuels my passion and has become my joyful purpose in life.

I now know that only when I learned to love myself first was it possible to attract someone who loves me for me. Happily married now to my best friend, a wonderful man who loves and accepts me for who I truly am—the good, the bad and the ugly—I know I don't have to lose myself to be in a relationship!

At our July Fourth wedding I wore a sexy red dress and sang "I love myself just the way I am!" I even wrote a verse for him: "I love you just the way you are!" It was the wedding of my dreams, done my way, with many of our 12-Step friends and family in attendance.

We spent our honeymoon in Alaska—we love to travel and experience the world together—and now work and play together in our new business, Passionate Joyful You! Together, we coach women to be who they are, and to celebrate their lives!

Today I have happy feet and dance my way through life, and the fireworks at my July Fourth wedding—echoed annually on that holiday—remind me that the day I gave my heart to someone who loves me for *me* was truly my Independence Day!

ABOUT THE AUTHOR: A Certified Transformational Dream Builder Coach and a Passion Test Facilitator, Charlotte uses her experience, joy and faith to help empower individuals, especially women, to discover their passions, recover their dreams, celebrate their true identity and live the life they love while shining their light and embracing their life's purpose. She is also an ordained minister, inspirational speaker, poet and seminar/workshop leader. A native Texan, Charlotte lives in Payson, AZ with her husband Keith who both are gypsies at heart. She is proud of her two grown children, four grand-children and two great-granddaughters.

Charlotte Beilgard
Passionate, Joyful and Prosperous YOU!
www.passionatejoyfulyou.com
passionatejoyfulyou@gmail.com
928-970-2177

My Journey With Dad
Judy Vartelas

I left college and headed home for Christmas break with no idea my life was about to change forever. Shortly after the holiday, I awakened early one morning to hear my dad yelling my name from the basement two floors below.

Instantly wide awake, a sense of dread came over me and I grabbed my robe. Adrenaline rushed through me as my body reacted to the energy of his voice. He'd just returned from the night shift at the local factory and seemed extremely upset. I ran down two flights of stairs and discovered my mother lying unconscious at the bottom.

Assuming she'd fainted, I tried to shake her awake. I touched her arms but pulled away immediately when I realized she was ice cold. I recognized her condition instantly but denial set in quickly, even as I attempted to make her more comfortable by grabbing a nearby pillow and gently resting her head upon it. The ambulance seemed to take forever and at one point I panicked.

"Why's it taking so long?" I asked the paramedic.

"I'm so sorry, but nothing can be done to save your mother," he replied, looking at me sadly." She'd had a massive heart attack and was gone.

At twenty-one, I'd lost my mother! She'd never be around to see me get married. My future children would never know her—be able to call her "Grandma." My first significant loss, I began to realize what the word "miss" really meant. Grief brought the difficult realization that once a loved one is taken by death, a part of me dies as well.

I attempted to return to college two weeks later without a mother in my life. I took a leave of absence for a semester and returned home after only a few weeks. Unable to function at school, I couldn't focus—never mind study. I needed time to process my profound sadness and grief. I had to wrap my head around the fact that for rest of my life I'd live without my mother. Grief and I became very intimate; it grabbed my heart and wouldn't let go.

Love Is Stronger Than Death

Death taught me the preciousness of life, and that I must never take a relationship I value for granted; life is just too fragile. Losing one parent made me aware that only one parent remained. I began to concentrate on developing a closer relationship with my dad, a kind, gentle man. One of eleven children from a large Greek family—his parents emigrated from Greece through Ellis Island and built a life here—he lived his whole life in our hometown.

A paratrooper during World War Two, after the war Dad obtained a job at the local factory down the street from our home. He drove a jitney there until his retirement. Dad always thought of others over himself. When we bought him his first snow blower, he'd come home early in the morning from work and plow the neighbors' sidewalks. He may have awakened a few neighbors at 3:30 a.m., but they never complained and always expressed gratitude.

No matter where I lived—from the time I attended graduate school two states away, got married, and began my life in New Jersey—Dad always visited with his white furry lapdog Misha for weeks at a time. I loved having him stay with us and appreciated my children's opportunity to spend quality time and make memories with their grandfather. We always looked forward to his visits.

The years passed, Dad retired, and it became evident that he'd aged and needed more care. Since my brother worked long hours and I ran a therapy practice from my home, we decided he'd move in with us. He settled in fairly well, loved to eat out with us, and enjoyed the kids' sports events. Whether it was a ride to his doctor or a meal my husband cooked for him, Dad never failed to let us know how much it meant to him. Always, he expressed appreciation and gratitude.

Soon Dad's health began to decline. I took him to the doctor, and as he was getting blood work the doctor spoke to me alone. He warned me to be careful—taking care of an elderly parent can be stressful. He reminded me of the importance of taking care of myself. I appreciated the doctor's input, but Dad was fairly independent so I wasn't overly concerned.

More years passed, and I became uncomfortable leaving him

alone for long periods of time and gave him a Life Alert. Often he'd fall when he got up in the middle of the night, and I'd settle him back into bed. Dad's falls exacerbated his arthritic pain and nighttime became taxing. Stoic, if Dad complained you knew he was really hurting. On my way out he'd thank me—even if it was three a.m., he was always grateful.

The Oxygen Mask

Juggling the care of an elderly parent, managing my private practice, and raising a family became overwhelming. Soon I was faced with choices. Often, taking care of Dad meant I'd be too tired to give of myself to my family. Exhaustion led to anemia as my body began to register stress internally. Guilt became my best friend, as the voices in my head told me I wasn't handling this very well.

My self-care changed drastically. Religious about going to the gym, now fatigue prevented me and I cancelled my membership. I reduced my daily meditations from twenty minutes to five, and napped whenever possible after staying up at night for Dad. I'm not sure when the stress began to overwhelm me, or exactly when I fell into total burnout, but as I plunged into an abyss of exhaustion everything seemed a heavy burden. I began to lose myself and my grip on the joy in my life. One night in bed I thought back to that doctor's warning about watching my own health as I cared for my dad. The instructions given to airplane passengers to put your own oxygen mask on first before helping another came to mind.

Shortly after, I attended a class on integrating spirituality and psychotherapy and was introduced to energy psychology, which addresses the relationship of an individual's energy systems to emotion, cognition, behavior, beliefs, and health. Applicable to a wide range of areas—including psychotherapy, education, pain management, sports, and peak performance—I was curious to see what it was really all about.

Skeptical at first—after using only traditional talk therapy for thirty years I decided to learn more about what seemed to be a very strange way to do therapy—the teacher chose me as a volunteer and instructed me to focus on something upsetting. I thought about my mother's death twenty years before and began to weep. I followed the teacher's directions and tapped acupuncture meridian points on my face and body. After each round, as I checked back into my body and emotions, my stress level declined. My tears stopped and by the end I felt amazingly calm and peaceful.

No Regrets

I believe there are no coincidences. On my way home that evening I knew something truly significant had happened! I couldn't wait to train further and apply these skills to my own stress.

Back home, when I left my Dad's room one night I was gripped by fear and panic, and began to sob heavily. Not only did I feel empathy for him, I worried about where he'd go if and when he needed greater care.

I began to apply these energy techniques throughout the day and de-stressed in a manner I didn't know was possible! Soon these techniques felt so good I didn't have to force myself to practice them. I used them when up late at night with Dad, and whenever I felt tired and disorganized. A life saver, energy psychology allowed me to begin on a pathway back home to myself!

Now when I experienced guilt I'd tap to release it from my system and move forward. As a result, I became more present for myself and others. At times I used it to rebalance my system, along with chakra clearing, and to help with my grief as Dad declined. I even taught Dad the exercises and practiced them along with him.

One particularly difficult night Dad fell in the bathroom and, after settling him back into bed, I felt sorry for myself. Exhausted, I had a mess to clean and needed to be up early for the kids the next day. Suddenly I realized that, if thoughts are energy, then my thoughts determine how I feel...

How can I transform my stress in this very moment? I wondered. I then attempted to change negative thoughts to positive as I continued to clean. *I'm so blessed to have an elderly parent to care for,* I realized, *especially since I never had the opportunity to watch my mother grow old! What a gift to watch Dad grow older and help him through!* Overwhelmed with appreciation, the task at hand became much easier as empowerment replaced defeat and reinforced my belief that good exists even in "bad" situations.

Epilogue

One Sunday when we returned from church, we found Dad lying on the kitchen floor, moaning in pain. While waiting for the ambulance I asked why he hadn't used his Life Alert.

"The front door was locked and I didn't want them to break through it—I figured you'd be home soon..." That was Dad, always thinking of others!

Shortly after, it became clear he needed care 24/7. I couldn't imagine how to tell Dad he wouldn't be coming home from the hospital with us. When I told him what the doctors recommended, it was one of the most difficult discussions of my life. He agreed, knowing he could no longer walk far, navigate stairs, or dress himself, and we both began to cry. I wanted to wave a magic wand and somehow make it all better.

"I don't want this to upset you," he said, as if our roles had suddenly reversed.

Dad is now ninety-six and on hospice care. I know he'll no longer be here to visit, hug, and kiss soon. I don't kid myself that I don't have the finality of grief ahead when I can no longer tell him in person how much I love him. I know I'll need the same energy tools when he is gone to assist me in completing this cycle of grief.

Meanwhile, I'm grateful he still recognizes me and the family, and is comforted by our presence during our visits. The best gift I can give Dad as he prepares to leave this lifetime is my never-ending love for him. I feel so blessed to have had my journey with Dad!

ABOUT THE AUTHOR: Judy Vartelas L.C.S.W., a Licensed Clinical Social Worker, Diplomate of Comprehensive Energy Psychology (DCEP), and a Nationally Certified Psychoanalyst (NCPSyA), maintains a thriving private practice and works with a wide variety of ages and issues. A prominent therapist since 1986, Judy works with clients on relationships, trauma, anxiety, depression, and performance enhancement. Judy lectures and provides training on the topic of energy psychotherapy at local universities and before general audiences, and is currently embarking on a course of study to become a life coach. Judy lives in New Jersey with her amazing family—husband Karl, daughter Alyssa, and son Spencer.

Judy Vartelas LCSW DCEP
www.CreateJoyWithin.com
Judy@CreateJoyWithin.com
973-838-0607

A Woman On The Mend

Kay Larrabee

"Now you will finally have a life!"

That was my mother's response to the news that I was getting married at the age of thirty. To my mother, a woman was not complete until she was wed. I suppose I bought into that belief a bit myself.

I know my family never expected me to marry. All my life, from an early age, I was told I was fat and unattractive. Yet looking back at photos of my youth, I was neither. A physical handicap put me in the hospital repeatedly as a child, and still limits my physical abilities to this day. My husband Allan claimed my limitations were not an issue, but I knew that was a lie when he left me.

"Would you leave me if I had an accident and became a paraplegic?" he once asked me.

"Of course not!" I replied.

And I didn't leave him through his sleep apnea, arthritis and knee degeneration, high blood pressure, severe eczema, or his workaholic behaviors. Nor did I bail on him through his bulimia and food addiction, which left him close to four hundred pounds. I saw him through bariatric surgery and recovery.

He lost almost two hundred pounds and left *me*.

After twenty years of marriage, Allan announced that he *was* getting a divorce. He'd already selected a lawyer, discussed the matter with his family, and withdrawn money from our savings account.

Completely blindsided by his announcement—never had we uttered the "D" word, even in our most difficult times—suddenly the life I'd known was over. In an instant, those four words—"I want a divorce"— changed my life forever. The future as I'd imagined it was gone. My relationship with Allan's family was gone. My partner was gone. I was completely alone.

Four words and I became a cliché'. I felt as if he'd kicked me in the gut, like I was falling down a bottomless pit, trying to hold on to something, anything—but there was nothing to stop my free fall down the hole. I felt like Alice in Wonderland—I just kept falling. I stayed in our house, afraid that Allan would change the locks if I traveled out of town to seek support from my family.

Completely devastated, it became clear this divorce was going to happen and I had no say in the matter. I couldn't stop it. Allan moved forward, filed divorce papers—served on me while working at a temporary job—and moved out of the house leaving me with our two mentally challenged teen-aged daughters. Quite a kick in the gut to be sued by the person you've trusted for more than twenty years...

Allan no longer contributed financially to the household, and paid no spousal or child support, but continued to take furniture piece by piece. Each day when I returned from my temporary job I'd find something else gone. He used funds from our joint checking account to pay his credit cards and rent, which left me very few funds to pay household expenses such as utilities and food. He disappeared for several months, reappearing only upon his return from a trip to Europe.

When I spoke to my brother about the impending divorce, his advice was to "hunker down." That's exactly what I did. I held two yard sales, sold my jewelry, and rolled all the loose change I could find. I placed an ad in our local newspaper to sell the remaining furniture that Allan hadn't already taken. I found a temporary full-time job to bring in a paycheck—even though it only lasted a few months. When I visited the safety deposit box at our bank, Allan had already been there and taken some of its contents.

The Fortune

When I look back on my marriage, I have to accept it hadn't been what I'd hoped for. Allan spent very little time with me or our adopted children. He was stingy with affection and often I had the feeling he resented me—though for what, I do not know.

So why would I stay in an unhappy relationship? Convinced I was damaged goods, I figured that no one else would ever want me. And so I persevered year after year.

I tried to be happy in my marriage. I busied myself with decorating our home, volunteering in our community, and pursuing a few business ideas. However, after a time I simply came to accept that this was my fate and that I was not destined to have happiness in my life. It just was not in the cards for me. I should be grateful that anyone wanted me at all.

When I spoke to my mother about my unhappiness during the marriage, she responded:

"Does he hit you? Does he gamble away the money? Does he drink away the money?"

I answered "no" to all of her questions.

"So what's your problem?" she asked.

About ten years into our marriage I opened a fortune cookie at a local Chinese buffet that read: *You Will Be Happy Late In Life.* I loved the happy part, but wasn't so thrilled about the late in life part! Would I find happiness on my deathbed? Would I have a couple years? Already in my forties, I wondered how late in life was "late?" I put that little slip of paper into my wallet and carried it with me for years. Every now and then I'd take it out, read it, and think: *When? When is my happiness coming?*

I had faith in that fortune. I had to. How else could I accept the unhappiness I felt? That fortune was telling me better days were ahead. And then those four words were spoken and Allan left. The children needed psychiatric hospitalization again. Everything I believed in was gone.

The divorce process dragged on and I had to travel to various court appearances and hearings. In the fall, I drove up to meet with my attorney and stayed at a local hotel alone. I'd forgotten about the fortune, but saw it in my wallet, pulled it out and read it now. *You Will Be Happy Late In Life,* it still said.

Ha! I laughed. *What a joke! I'm already fifty-one years old—how late is it going to be?*

Next I fell to my knees beside the bed and clasped my hands in prayer, though to this day I don't know why I reacted this way. But instead of asking God for help or why this was happening to me, I found myself speaking words of gratitude.

"Thank you, thank you!" I cried out. Despite the severe challenges I continued to face as I proceeded through a contentious divorce, I knew in my heart that my life was better now than it had been in my marriage.

The Road To Happiness

After our house sold, I slept on an air mattress in the apartment

I rented and pinched pennies by unplugging lamps, my computer, and the printer before I went to bed. I lived on milk, cheap white bread, eggs, cheese, and pasta—lots of pasta. I went through our house collecting toiletries left in the bathrooms, and packing up non-perishable food from our pantry and emergency food closet to take to my new place. I didn't even allow myself to purchase a Sunday newspaper. Yet, despite all of this, I was grateful.

And then I had a revelation. What if *this* was my way to happiness? Was this divorce what I had to go through to find to the happiness proclaimed in that fortune cookie so long ago? I decided to believe that it was. And every time I received a summons to appear in court, or contentious petitions from opposing counsel, I took a deep breath and reminded myself: *You are on the road to your happiness.*

I'd like to say it was easy from then on. But challenges remained. I had to appear at several court hearings and be cross-examined by my spouse's divorce attorney, whose job was to make me look bad whatever way he could. My two teenage daughters were in a juvenile probation facility and psychiatric facility, respectively, so there were meetings for them as well.

Finally, my divorce was over, but not before I received a breast cancer diagnosis. I underwent a lumpectomy followed by seven weeks of radiation therapy. Fortunately, my family rallied around me and my two older sisters and I spent time together. I found gratitude once again as I sat in the oncologist's waiting room where I saw other patients who were not as lucky as me.

The Silver Lining

So what did my road to happiness look like now? I had to be rejected by my spouse of twenty years, lose my relationship with my in-laws, my house, my kids, my identity, my security, my career, and experience a health crisis. I had to let go of everything I believed to be true, and lose everything I thought was important.

I felt that if I didn't find something positive to bring out of this devastating journey, it would have all been for naught. It would also mean that my ex-spouse had won, and I was not going to let that happen. I decided to pay it forward. I stopped caring about what others thought about me, including my family, and created a unique business called *Women on the Mend Divorce Concierge Services* that works with women experiencing challenging and unexpected loss in their lives—whether a relationship or a job.

Was this the journey I would have chosen? Of course not! But it was what I had to do just the same. We rarely get to decide what our journey—meant to get us where we're supposed to be in this life—will look like. The only thing under our control is how we deal with that journey—rough though it may be.

There is a second fortune cookie—found when I was undergoing my radiation treatments. It said: *Your Success Will Astonish Everyone.* I've decided to have faith in this fortune as well, as I continue to be a woman—and help *other* women—on the mend...

ABOUT THE AUTHOR: Kay Larrabee, Founder of WOMEN ON THE MEND, is a Certified Career Coach and a woman who has been through the trials and tribulations of the divorce process. She has dedicated herself to using her Career Coaching skills and firsthand experience with divorce to guide others through these difficult life transitions. As a speaker, Kay shares her knowledge and experience with others, admits the mistakes she made during the divorce process and presents a plan that will help others, not only protect their financial future, but move through this traumatic time with empowerment and grace.

Kay Larrabee
Women On The Mend
www.TheDivorceConciergeOfSouthJersey.com
womenonthemend@hotmail.com
856-628-5272

Jumping *For* Joy
And *With* Joy!

Sheri Horn Hasan

I shuffle the small *Mirror Cards* deck, spread the cards face down on the table, and randomly pick one.

"Joy," it reads. "Joy is only possible when we surrender to the richness of the moment."

How weird, I think. *I'm at the tail-end of my four and-a-half year relationship with John and I pull the "Joy" card?* It's been only the past week or so that I've accepted that it's finally, truly, utterly over. Ironically, the only relationship I've ever experienced joy over ending was that with my ex-husband. Ten mostly joyless years married (and three semi-joyous years prior to the wedding) were punctuated only by the ecstatic joy-filled entrance of our son into our lives.

That relationship was one built around control, lack of communication, and unexpressed expectations, and I initiated my divorce happily because it meant freedom from such restriction. *This* relationship was one of two post-divorced "been there, done that" individuals who shunned the notion that relationships must always deteriorate and disintegrate in the end as long as compatibility, respect, and courtesy comprise the cornerstones of true togetherness—with a high dose of sexual attraction thrown in, of course.

Or so I thought...sigh...

The Beginning Of The End

"What do you mean you'd rather spend New Year's Eve with your son than with me?" I asked John, the hurt in my voice obvious.

"Well, no, it's not that—I don't—I mean, it's his friend's parents' party and they're only inviting a few people," John responded defensively. "And besides, Stephanie can't accompany Matt, so I'm his 'one-plus!'"

"So, you're saying that you'd rather be your son's 'date' than do something with me, or invite me along as well?" *Pretty obvious slap in the face, if you ask me,* I think...but I respond: "Well, I guess if that's what you want, then go ahead. Just recognize that I'm not sure how I'll feel about you after the fact..."

I was being honest. I'd been rejected before—in some ways it was the story of my life—and I sensed this was a pivotal point in our relationship. At the same time, I couldn't force him to do something he didn't want to. I hated making anyone feel obligated, and clearly he didn't value being with me on the holiday, though for the life of me I couldn't figure out why.

We'd always been pretty loose about holidays, since we both had teenagers who lived in different towns and hung out with different friends. So we shared holidays together when convenient, but spent time with our own kids when it wasn't. Now his kids had turned eighteen and nineteen, while my son was seventeen and spending New Year's Eve with his dad. This holiday was a no-brainer, I thought.

Upset, I looked again at the transits to my natal astrological chart. A professional astrologer, I'd cringed when I'd seen the planet Saturn transiting opposite my natal sun several months before, as the classic interpretation of this is the end of a relationship. I know the universe is benign and always operates in our best interest, and that it gives us not necessarily what we *want*, but rather what we *need*—but did I really *need* to lose this relationship? And, if so, *why?*

Since Saturn represents the authoritarian parent from our childhood, I knew the manifestation of the energies inherent in its opposition to my natal sun represented an attempt to teach me about behavior patterns that required examination right now. Saturn—known to be one of the most important planets to watch as it makes its twenty-nine and a half year cycle around one's natal chart and "touches" planets or sensitive points there—*always* means serious business and *never* fools around. I knew I was being asked to "own" my inner authority, but I remained in the dark about exactly how to do that *and* prevent the loss of my relationship with John at the same time.

My Heart Belongs To Daddy

The truth is I've always attracted men who are emotionally unavailable. I *know* this, yet the pattern never seemed to change!

But this relationship was different, I lamented, *it was supposed to be the real thing!*

Maybe I only felt that way because—already in my late forties when we met—I'd experienced marriage, and figured it was now about finding someone with whom mutual attraction *and* true compatibility coexisted. *I thought we had that—what went wrong?* I beat myself up with this question and, as usual, these kinds of thoughts brought me back to my relationship with my father.

Nearly seventeen years after his sudden death at age sixty-nine due to complications from chemotherapy, my father's loss still loomed large in my life. A brilliant, emotionally elusive man who taught mathematics and physics at Wagner College in Staten Island, N.Y., for thirty-five years, my father ran a tight ship at home. I idolized him, even though he proved to be a benevolent dictator. I remember how arguing with him in my childhood when my brother and I wanted to stay up an extra half an hour to watch the end of some television show proved futile. The answer was always "no!" And he meant it.

My father operated the planetarium at Wagner for a few years and taught courses on astronomy. My tenth birthday party included a trip to the planetarium for a private show, which at the time everyone considered way cool...

He used to give me books about Greek mythology that told timeless archetypal stories about the origin of the many constellations—ones he'd point out as they'd shine so beautifully, illuminated against the backdrop of the nighttime sky. He introduced me to individual stars and the meanings behind them. Betelgeuse, Aldebaran, and Sirius were household words during my youth.

He taught me also the meaning of the word "googol"—the number "one" followed by a hundred zeros, and "googolplex,"—a googol multiplied by itself, which needless to say, is quite a large number. One year I found a birthday card for him that said "I love you a googolplex!" Pleased, he chuckled as I beamed from ear to ear, pleased at myself for pleasing him.

It took until after his death when I was thirty-eight to understand how lost I felt without him. Gregarious and eclectic, he was a natural teacher. Students either loved him or hated him, but always he was his authentic self. A family man, he was nevertheless too bright not to have outside interests, and by the time I reached my early teens he devoted many hours to running Wagner's ice hockey club and worked as a statistician for the National Hockey League's New Jersey Devils. In short, often he wasn't around, and I found myself tagging along at times just to feel included in his life...

Raised in the Jewish faith, my father was a "Kohen," or descendant of the high holy priests of the Temple of Jerusalem. Throughout Judaic history, the designation Kohen is passed from father to son hereditarily, and among its distinctions is that they are the first to be called up during Torah readings in temple. Though females are not accorded the same distinction, I always understood myself to be a proud Kohen descendant regardless.

You *Can* Go Back Again

Two years ago I began to study past life regression. I wanted to learn about my own past life karma and to facilitate regressions for others. I enrolled in a series of modules in Deep Memory Process regression work, a methodology pioneered by Roger Woolger and taught by DMP practitioner and evolutionary astrologer Patricia Walsh.

DMP is based on the principle that at death, when the soul leaves the body and attempts to ascend in order to reincarnate, it carries with it "cellular memory" from the body it is vacating. For example, if one died violently in a past life, the imprints left on the body remain with the soul despite reincarnation. Regression work is healing because it reveals how a person died and can explain why we experience specific emotional blocks in this lifetime.

During my regression I saw myself as a young woman circa the mid-1800's in my mother's house taking care of her as she lay dying. Somehow I knew my father had passed years before. She dies, and I realize I've dedicated my twenties to caring for her, never taking the opportunity to leave, marry, and raise a family of my own. I'm left with the house as my inheritance, and some money in the bank. Nad've, all I know is that I have no parents or family and some gold coins in the bank.

Alone and depressed, I walk to town (our house is on the other side of a small wooded area, separated from the main town— strangely similar to my childhood home in this lifetime) to visit the banker and request my inheritance to take home. I saw myself walking through town carrying a small burlap bag filled with gold coins—my parent's entire life savings, now mine.

As I reach the edge of the woods, suddenly I'm attacked from behind. Three men have seen me nonchalantly carrying my bag of gold and decided to rob me. One man grabs me from behind and, surprised, I drop the bag. The other two scramble to retrieve the bag of coins, and I break free and run through the woods into the clearing that leads to my house. All three chase me across the clearing in hot pursuit, determined to leave no witness to their crime. They catch up with me, throw me to the ground, and suffocate me.

Now, as I reflect upon the end of my current relationship, suddenly I realize with stark clarity that I've never fully honored my own "gold"—a metaphor for my inner strengths and talents—in this lifetime! Saturn's been saying: Don't *devalue* your own true gifts, passed down to you by your father—*respect* your intrinsic value, *integrate* it into your core self and *stop* taking it for granted!

And in that instant it dawns on me: I'd never perceived what I possessed internally to be worth protection! Suddenly I realize I *must* understand my own true worth *and* protect what is mine. I can no longer treat casually my own true gifts. When I do, I remain uncommitted to myself, and then manifest around me those who cannot commit to me! After all, how can they when I fail to make the inner commitment to fully appreciate myself?

I marvel at this revelation, pick up the "Joy" card once again, and read: "Maybe you're questioning where the joy is in your relationship, but chances are that this situation is familiar to you, even from when you were single. For joy is not 'out there.' It's in you, and always has been...young children jump *for* joy and *with* joy..."

Suddenly I totally *get it:* My gold *is* my joy—it's my true treasure within...*L'Chaim!*

ABOUT THE AUTHOR: Writing coach, editor, and professional astrologer Sheri Horn Hasan utilizes her 30+ years editing experience and deep intuition to help bring authors' individual stories to life through her company *Karmic Evolution Publishing.* Editor of the Powerful You! *Women Living Consciously* anthology series, Sheri has helped 100+ authors realize their dream to publish! Have a book idea? *Contact Sheri today!* Separately, Sheri coaches clients interested in astrology as a tool for greater consciousness and soul growth how to move from chaos to clarity and co-create their own futures through astrological insight! Learn more about her astrological services at *Karmic Evolution Astrology!*

Sheri Horn Hasan
Editor and Astrologer
www.KarmicEvolution.com
info@KarmicEvolution.com
732-547-0852

Bumps In The Road

Mary L. Brogdon

Why is it I don't always have the experience of joyfulness? I wonder. After all, I drive a car with a license plate that reads IMJOIFL! So why do I need reminders to experience the joy in my life?

I have asked my higher self what blocks come between me and my expression of joy. The answers to that question have to do with conquering, or at least managing, some of my inner demons. I acknowledge some thought patterns and behavioral patterns in me that limit my joy.

Before *Sesame Street* aired in 1966, before there were color television sets, there was a television program for pre-school children called *Romper Room School.* It ran from 1953 to 1994. Even though I was already in grade school in 1953, I watched *Romper Room* during my school vacations. The *Romper Room* teacher utilized helpers called Do Bees and Don't Bees to illustrate her lessons, which were brought to life with drawings of Do Bees and Don't Bees, or by someone dressed in a bee costume.

In one video I found recently on YouTube, the teacher says: "Do Bee a chair sitter. Don't Bee a chair tilter." This particular video comes from Australia, and as I write this, I can hear the actress speaking in her Australian accent using perfect diction. She describes to the children both acceptable and unacceptable behavior for sitting in their chairs. Then she leads the class in a song that goes like this: "I always do what's right. I never do anything wrong. I'm a *Romper Room* Do Bee. I Do Bee all day long."

The message of that song is imbedded into my brain. Always do things right, all day long, be a good girl. First it's do right, then be good, and that leads to having approval. My childhood was not unique in this respect. However, my need to be perfect—always do what's right, never do anything wrong—makes it difficult to live in joy.

Romper Room was not my first introduction to the concept of "always do what's right," but it illustrates a prevailing theme throughout my formative years. My mother once told me that when I was learning to talk, with each new word added to my vocabulary, my father insisted I repeat the new word until I could say it perfectly. Perfectionism is one block to my awareness of the joy in my life.

Joy Stealers

For almost thirty years now, I've subscribed to a different philosophy that teaches I was born perfect—perfect, whole and complete. To feel joy and know peace, I need only remember that I am already perfect and there is nothing for me to do. Humph! I get that conceptually—I can even stay mindful of it for a few minutes at a time, but then I slip back into habitual ways of thinking. Perfectionism is like a disease, and if left untreated, it leads to another limiting behavior pattern—another of my inner demons—the self-defeating habit of procrastination.

Procrastination blocks my joy because I can't be present in the moment when I know there is something I need to do, but instead of getting it done I put it off or try to avoid it all together. Procrastination is a pattern that's very similar to an addiction. It's an inner demon that I constantly need to manage. It doesn't help that there's some attention deficit disorder (ADD) in the mix. These ADD tendencies became apparent to me in the past ten to fifteen years and—as the amount of sensory input has increased exponentially over that period of time—seems more noticeable to me now. Or maybe I'm simply more aware. I do pay more attention now to my inner knowing...

Earlier in my life, I wanted to be the perfect mom, perfect wife, and perfect caregiver, so perfection was part of my theme throughout, and I guess why I was so miserable, in my first marriage. It was far from perfect! Married for eight years, Larry was based in the military in Hawaii and I was in Texas when I sent him a "Dear John" letter asking for a divorce. I wanted Larry to be perfect, or at least try to resolve the conflicts and go to counseling with me, but he wouldn't even do that until the very end. Shortly after receiving my letter, he had a stroke and they sent him home to work out his marital problems.

We divorced and they say he never fell out of love with me. Just because we were divorced didn't mean we weren't in each other's lives, especially since we had two children together. I remarried two years after our divorce, and was married for twenty-four years. After my second husband died, Larry asked if I'd move back to Texas and live with him; he wanted us to re-marry. Not me...

The Sacred Assignment

I had to continually remind myself—almost on a daily basis—that I chose this...I volunteered for it, was committed to it, and had to find a way to make the best of it! Though one of the most depressing tasks I've taken on in a long time, I thought there'd be some overall lesson, some completion of karmic debt...

My daughter Jennifer and I took on what I now call the "sacred assignment" for several months in 2012 when we teamed up to care for Larry, her ailing father and my ex-husband. Divorced thirty-three years, this was not an easy task for me. Long standing tension between Jenny and her father made it that much more difficult. And it wasn't easy for Larry because he no longer had complete control of his life.

Instead, he had not one but two bossy women telling him what he should and shouldn't do, could and couldn't do, and when. We worked hard to make it work. Larry still loved me, and he loved Jenny and our son Michael also, but his way of showing it sometimes made us crazy. It felt manipulative, controlling, and oppressive, yet at the same time we recognized he wanted to make our lives easier. It didn't feel easier to us. His declining health and impaired cognition interfered with his ability to manage his own life.

Jenny managed his finances and personal affairs. It took both of us, working with the Veterans Administration, to manage his healthcare. I was his nurse, case manager and twenty-four-hour attendant. A hospice case manager for the last sixteen years of my career, I'd been in hundreds, maybe thousands of people's homes, and dozens of assisted living and nursing homes in Orange Country, California. Well-versed in home care situations with what works and what doesn't, both Jenny and Larry wanted my help.

As lovable and easy-going as this man could be, he proved equally frustrating to live with and care for. Jenny and I commiserated daily about how difficult he made life for us. Of course, the more we talked about our misery, the worse it got.

A challenging time for our family, I did what was necessary for Jenny's sake. She wouldn't have been able to do it without my help. Our united effort brought the two of us closer. And, as challenging and draining as it was, there was joy in the experience—in the teamwork, the forgiveness after the fighting—and there was laughter when we shared a comical moment over something he said or did that day.

Being home, most days I took pleasure in the beauty of nature that surrounded our house—the flowers, green grass, and huge old pepper tree outside my patio door. Its open canopy permitted sunlight to filter through its leaves, and its thick gnarled branches spanned twenty feet in all directions, high above the rooftop. I appreciated the birds, hummers, butterflies, and squirrels nearby.

During this trying time, I sought additional tools to open myself to joy. I nurtured myself with massages, and drew strength from my spiritual community and the hugs and kisses received there from positive, like-minded people who I allowed to love and support me. I took great pleasure in expressing myself through music and found joy singing with the church choir. Singing always raises my vibration and puts me in a joyful mood. I found joy in volunteering my services at my spiritual center where I learned a new skill working in the audio-visual booth during Sunday services.

Sad, mad, and depressed about our situation for months, Jenny and I remained committed to it for as long as Larry remained conscious. When he developed pneumonia for the third time in three months, the doctor ordered hospice care and within a week our patient died.

Feeling Uplifted Now

I continue now to become more awake and aware as part of my spiritual journey. I incorporate spiritual practices into my life that involve reading, journaling, praying, meditating, and affirmations. I speak my vision statement into the universe, and compose a gratitude and "To Be" list. No longer practicing to make perfect, I recognize these practices for the sole benefit of having a practice.

My "To Be" list might read: "Today I intend to be loving, kind, compassionate, and forgiving of myself and others. I am a beneficial presence in my world. I see God in me; I greet the God in all others." I tag on this short saying from a *Creative Thought* magazine that I memorized some twenty years ago:

Enthusiasm is my byword
Joy is my chosen mood
Wisdom is my guide
Love is my purpose
Fulfillment is my reward
God is my source.

Joy, I believe, is found in present moment situations. God once shared with me that FUN is really an acronym for "feeling uplifted now." And it is challenging to be here now. Sometimes I use that as my mantra in meditation: "Be here now."

I take comfort in the knowledge that I am a work in progress. And what a piece of work I am! I am learning to love myself and my life just the way it is, and just the way it is not. To that end, I will continue to manage those limiting and unproductive thoughts and habit patterns until no longer necessary, using the tools I've gained and learning new ones. I will associate with like-minded people whenever and wherever possible because I know I can't do it alone. And the good news is...I'm never alone. Thank you, God.

I've identified road blocks to my awareness of joy's presence in my life, and see how my journey to joy is fraught with multiple stops and starts, similar to driving the freeways of Los Angeles during rush hour. I've encountered detours and roundabouts, as well as long stretches of highway across the desert without a place to stop for rest, refreshment, or refueling. I've met with circumstances where lives collide with upset, much like a traffic accident. Suffice it to say, I have survived the many bumps in the road...

ABOUT THE AUTHOR: Mary Brogdon devoted the last sixteen years of her forty-year nursing career to end-of-life care as a hospice nurse. She observed that most people die in the same way as they live. A great set of life skills makes a difference. Upon retirement from nursing, Mary's focus shifted from helping clients die well to helping them live well. She teaches life mastery skills based upon principles of ancient spiritual wisdom. She coaches clients in transforming their dreams into reality through the practical application of spiritual principles. She founded TLC Connection, where TLC means Tender Loving Choices.

Mary L Brogdon
TLC Connection
www.TenderLovingChoices.com
mary@TenderLovingChoices.com
714-624-4368

Chaos To Clarity
Lily J. Lee

I awaken in a pool of cold sweat and rush to the bathroom in a panic. My hands are cold and clammy, my feet frozen as ice. I look in the mirror and see a ghastly pale image of myself, as if I'm slowly fading away...*how did this happen?* is all I can think...*one minute madly in love, the next instant it's over?*

Of course, nothing "just happens," but then again, this seems an old story. Boy meets girl—falls head over heels. Love develops over the years and fizzles slowly through a series of unforeseen events. *How could I have been so foolish—to let myself believe in everlasting love? I feel like I've wasted so many years of my life...*

My awakening from chaos to clarity started the moment I realized my marriage was over. Pitch black, the room's darkness matched my mood. Chilled by the hopeless thoughts that ran through my mind, my loneliness was pervasive. It seemed my only source of comfort—surprisingly—came in the form of my sobs.

Though I'd never thought about it until that moment, my upset and disappointment alerted me to the fact that my world was coming to an end! Devastated, the flood of emotions made me sick. Queasy, empty, and sad, I felt like a failure.

Maybe we lacked enough open and honest communication. Perhaps this led to a dearth of special quality moments shared by couples in order to intimately reconnect after a hard day. At some point, we stopped sharing—making eye contact, holding hands—and soon thereafter no longer noticed each other as lovingly as before. Affection is important to me and when soft caresses and words of love and support no longer existed, it became increasingly difficult.

I remember those desperate sleepless nights of waiting for him. How I longed for some kind of *anything* to happen. We grew apart and my frustration increased. I felt helpless, as though I was watching a train wreck happen in slow motion. I knew it was coming but couldn't do anything about it.

Maybe it was the sadness and loneliness. Or the pain of my heart being ripped out and crushed into a million pieces. Either way, it was the fear—of rejection, of abandonment, and, well, of being afraid—that made it clear to me I needed a change.

Shattered Dreams

For me, my journey begins from a place of love. As a little girl, I always believed in fairytales. I pictured meeting Prince Charming and riding blissfully off into the sunset. I envisioned my beautiful white wedding gown on a gorgeous picturesque day. In a perfect setting, magnificent flowers bloom with a slight hint of violet. Family and friends gather to witness a ceremony filled with sunshine and smiles. It did, in fact, turn out to be one of the most incredible and unforgettable moments of my life.

I recalled the countless experiences of joy, like the first time he made me smile. Or the time we walked on the beach and couldn't stop talking and laughing. Our wonderful talks were timeless. Young, we had a plan and wanted to share the rest of our lives together. One night when we looked up at the crystal clear sky, we knew we had it all—our future was bright and everything lay ahead of us.

My fairytale romance would last a lifetime, or so I thought. Especially since I was focused and determined! I didn't know then that love was not enough and that one hundred percent effort means different things to different people. I really truly believed that neither one of us entered matrimony with ill will—we both took our marriage vows seriously and with good intention.

My fifteen year marriage resulted in three healthy, beautiful children. Together we created our little gifts from God and I love each child immensely—they are my greatest joy. So at first my constant thought was to keep my family together. Many times I kept my mouth shut just to keep the peace. Yet every time I made a sacrifice to do this, I felt like I was losing a part of my soul. What was the fighting about anyway? Control? Fear? Discontentment?

It took me a long time to come to terms with my new reality. At first I tried my best to be a good wife, mother, and daughter, and divorce was the furthest thing from my mind. But as time went on, my every effort went unacknowledged. Knowing this was daunting, because I was experiencing the roughest time in my life as I juggled the care of my parents in between childcare activities. The despair and disconnect of my marriage became too much to bear.

I tried everything in my power and exhausted all possible

avenues to bring back the spark that had once ignited our marriage. But attempts to spend quality time together only made things worse. While sitting through an audio marriage therapy session, he began to snore and continued from start to finish. A last ditch effort, it became quite obvious that he'd checked out and didn't plan to stick around. My feeling of being taken for granted—like a comfortable, boring piece of furniture—was secondary only to my feelings of betrayal. This cut so deep it may leave scars that take a lifetime to heal.

Finally, it was obvious that things seemed to be coming to an end. All those sleepless nights of wondering what will be. Never had I thought I'd be a woman who quit. My motto, after all, is "never quit!" But so is "living life to the fullest authentically..." That became my true dilemma: Do I pretend to be happy as my resentment and bitterness toward my husband grows?

Many people frown upon the chaos of a divorce and believe in staying in a marriage for the sake of the children. *But at what cost? I wondered, the cost of freedom to feel alive? The cost of having my children witness and cultivate an environment full of lies? That's not fair to them.* I believe that creating a healthy home where loving and honest feelings and behaviors are nurtured and exhibited is more important. Children have a right to live peacefully surrounded by lots of love and support. This is optimal whether parents are together or apart.

One lesson I've learned thus far is that, when the struggles begin, strength comes from within. As I continued to spiral deeper into depression, I saw a glimmer of hope, a renewed understanding that I could achieve my greatest joy if only I could let go. Letting go is the hardest thing I had to accomplish.

Sacred Spaces

I held my father's hands and looked into his teary eyes. I whispered in his ear, told him how much he meant to me, how I appreciated all the years he'd been there for me unconditionally, and how much I loved him. Dying of cancer right in front of my eyes— though he'd fought valiantly for a few years despite originally being told he had only three months to live—his final departure left me devastated.

A remarkable man—full of life, love, and lots of laughter—he'd clung to every breath to stay with us a little longer. He valued his family and was always passionate, generous, and considerate. He hung on to receive his last rites, gave my hand a strong squeeze, and took his last breath.

Our family said goodbye and we cried because we were sad, but also out of happiness for him. It was bittersweet. He was no longer suffering, and he left peacefully. His love, laughter, and joy made everyone's life he touched better.

Death and change, though painful, are necessary parts of life. Now I realize that if I could survive my father's illness and death, and incorporate within all of those wonderful qualities he embodied when alive, I will always carry a piece of him and his legacy inside of me.

My hope is to never lose my childlike wonder. I still believe in "happily ever after" because I have faith and believe that it exists. I pray each day and appreciate the blessings in my life. I know that as long as there is hope for a new beginning, love survives in each and every one of us. I cherish my children's laughter—it has made me realize that the only way I can receive joy is to forgive myself and willingly let go. Only then is it possible for me to move on into peace and everlasting love. I always remember that I am my father's living legacy...

As difficult as my divorce is, I understand that the misery leading to the end of my marriage will—through the process of transformation—bring me ultimately to a place of renewed hope for love and a brighter future...from chaos to clarity...

ABOUT THE AUTHOR: Lily J. Lee is a dynamic Visionary, resourceful Go-getter with a "Never Quit" attitude. She is an Entrepreneur and Founder & CEO of Optimum Coach, specializing in business success and leadership coaching. Lily's passion is to teach, motivate, and empower her clients to pursue an authentic and meaningful purpose aligned with their personal and professional vision. She holds an M.S. degree in Organizational Leadership, and has an extensive background in legal research, real estate, sales, marketing, business development and management. Lily helps entrepreneurs and businesses increase sales and profits through customized strategies towards achieving successful results!

Lily J. Lee
Optimum Coach
www.optimumcoach.com
info@optimumcoach.com
516-200-1180

PART THREE

Follow Your
Passion

*"The personal life, deeply lived,
expands into truths beyond itself."*
~ Anais Nin

Dusting Off Old Dreams ~ Yes, I Am!

Sarah Bernardi Carkner

"I'm gonna live forever, I'm gonna learn how to fly—High!
I feel it coming together, people will see me and cry—Fame!
I'm gonna make it to heaven, light up the sky like a flame—Fame!"
~ Theme Song from the Movie "Fame"

Every Wednesday night I'd throw myself at my mother's feet, wrap my arms around her ankles, and look up at her with pleading puppy dog eyes. "*Please* let me eat in front of the T.V. tonight?" I'd implore her.

I was seven years old in 1982 and would just *die* if I missed one second of the opening credits of my favorite T.V show during which Erica Gimbel (a.k.a. Coco Hernandez) sang the Academy Award-winning Best Original Song "Fame!" Based heavily on the Fiorello H. LaGuardia High School of Music & the Arts and the High School of Performing Arts in New York City, I dreamed of being like one of the show's main characters—Coco, Leroy, Doris, and Bruno. I fantasized that one day I'd break out in song in the middle of the street, dance on cafeteria tables, and just as the lyrics suggested "light up the sky like a flame!"

Luckily, I didn't have to die those Wednesday nights from 1982 to 1987 when the program aired, as my merciful mother exempted me from her cardinal rule of eating family dinner together. She also signed me up for dance classes.

After a few years of dance classes, the owner of the studio announced that we were invited to a dance convention in New York City. I pirouetted with excitement—I was going to the city in which the school that inspired me to dance was located! To top it off, my teacher announced that my dance-mate Melissa and I would be put into the advanced group at the convention. I puffed a bit at the idea. *I must be pretty good if I'm going into the advanced group!* I thought proudly.

On the edge of my seat during the two-hour car ride to the Big Apple, I bubbled over with anticipation. We pulled up to the New York Sheraton Hotel and it seemed like a hundred lights illuminated the entranceway. Dance signs adorned the windows, people bustled in and out of the revolving doors, and music greeted us as we entered the hotel.

We hurried to our first class of the day; my heartbeat quickened and my stomach fluttered. Just before we reached our destination, one of the chaperones turned to Melissa and I and whispered "girls, I just want to let you know this first class is also an audition for a Dance Caravan that picks out children to perform across the country!"

Immediately I imagined what it would be like to dance on various stages across the country—if I made the troop my flame would certainly light up the sky!

Melissa grabbed my hand and snapped me out of my daydream. We looked each other in the eye and, as ten year-old girls do, screamed at a pitch akin to the mermaid screech in the classic 80's movie "Splash." We regained our composure, took a deep breath, and opened the door to all of the possibilities that lay ahead...

Big Fish in a Little Pond

There must have been more than two hundred dancers moving simultaneously to the music that blared from the enormous speakers above. Everyone moved around me, but I froze—I had no idea where to go or what to do. Totally overwhelmed and with no one giving us directions, Melissa and I scurried up to the front of the room and attempted to join in.

The instructors on the platform illustrated a series of dance steps and we were expected to immediately pick up the moves and follow them. I'd never done this before! At our studio back home we were shown the moves slowly—in fact two or three times. Here in New York, I simply couldn't keep up! Flabbergasted, Melissa looked at me—she couldn't keep up either...

We retreated to the side of the room, removing ourselves from the crowd. I sunk down to the ground with my back against the wall, and watched the other dancers move effortlessly across the floor.

Totally unprepared, I felt completely defeated. New York may be the city where dreams are made, but at that moment my dream was crushed. Back home I was a big fish in a little pond. In New York I didn't even feel like plankton!

Everything after that experience seemed to reinforce my belief that I couldn't pursue dancing professionally. When I accompanied my father on a business trip to Yale University and we entered the gothic-style science building, he escorted me to the sidewall that displayed a large black and white map of the campus. A physicist who worked with medical technologies, he pointed to the medical building and said "when you're older, you are going to study here!"

"No," I replied, "I'm going here!" I pointed to the dance building.

"No," he retorted, "you have scientific aptitude Sarah—you should go here!"

A total daddy's little girl, I folded and said "sure, dad." I didn't want to disappoint him. *He probably doesn't think I could be a dancer anyway,* my pre-teen angst told me as I walked away slowly. Back at home, I relayed to my mother the verbal exchange that had taken place.

"Sarah, aren't dancers tall and thin?" she responded. Coming from an Italian family whose motto is "food is love," and whose women are—on average—five feet two inches tall, my mother's words served to totally extinguish any ember of hope left in my dream to light up the sky up like a flame.

By high school, dancing became a hobby and not a career pursuit. I put my "childish" dream of going to the High School of Performing Arts on the shelf—along with my "Fame" records—and left them to collect dust. I embraced my scientific aptitude and headed off to college.

Dreams Are Forever!

Still, I had the need to move. To fulfill this, and to earn some extra cash, I began teaching group exercise classes. Over the next decade I leapt from one fitness trend to the next...but always, I missed dancing. When a new fitness and health club opened in the area, I approached the aerobics director to ask if I could teach a dance-based fitness class. After an audition that went much better than the one in New York, I was hired.

Excited to combine my love of dance and fitness, I dove in with enthusiasm. Though a bit rusty, developing choreography ignited an internal excitement I hadn't felt in years! I began to reclaim a lost quality in myself that I'd denied for way too long. While teaching my first dance fitness class, I looked out at the participants and watched as smiles lit up their faces. The energy in that room had me flying high!

"Are you a dancer?" asked one class member who approached me afterward. "You must be a dancer to move like that!" The poor woman had no idea what a loaded question this was. I truly didn't know how to respond.

"Well, sort of," I replied.

A year later the aerobics director asked to speak with me. This was out of character and, since she'd never asked to speak with me before, I felt like a schoolgirl called to the principal's office. Maybe she caught me not wearing my fitness team shirt! With much trepidation I opened her tiny office door. I sat on her bench, smiled nervously, and said "what can I do for you?"

"Sarah I'd like to start a new dance fitness program, and I can't do it without you—you're a great dancer!" she smiled. "You have the moves and know how to put them together!" I relaxed and, thankful that I wasn't getting reprimanded for my attire, let out a sigh of relief.

"To keep up with the hottest fitness trends I'd like you to teach a dance fitness class with a sexier edge," she continued. "You're an all-American girl—you have real boobs and are very approachable."

I almost fell off the bench laughing. I'd never thought of myself in that way!

"That's hysterical!" I replied. "Of course I'll do it!"

I may have walked away from my passion once, but that didn't mean it was gone forever—now it looked like it had come back around to give me a second chance! From that moment on I decided to let go of the limiting beliefs I'd created around the idea of what constitutes a real dancer. *I don't need anyone's approval to dance,* I thought. *I don't need to be tall and thin—I just need to dance for me!*

I vowed to no longer minimize what I could accomplish, or the goals I could attain, and realized that if others could "light up the sky like a flame" there's no reason why I couldn't too! So I dusted off my dream to "live forever" and "learn how to fly high," and recognized that my path there was simply a different one.

Now I say: If you have a song inside your soul, sing it! If you have a story to tell, begin it! If you have an image inside your mind, paint it! It's never too late to reconnect with your passion!

Since then, I've dusted off my old "Fame" records, and as I listen to them my eyes well up with tears. It takes courage to be who you really are, and I guess I just needed to grow into myself. Besides, the dance floor would be very dull if no one went on it except those that moved the best.

Now, at the end of class when a participant asks me "are you a dancer?" I say with renewed confidence: "Why yes—yes, I am!"

ABOUT THE AUTHOR: Sarah Carkner obtained her Bachelors in Neuroscience and Masters of Wellness Management while also pursuing her love of dance and fitness. An advocate of personal growth and self-development, Sarah is a Certified Professional Coach with a successful business and life coaching practice. Sarah has established herself as a local fitness expert and recently co-founded F.A.B Women Fitness®. Sarah has appeared as a guest expert on "Navigating Your Life with Nat Williams," and presented at over 25 venues in the tri-state area ranging from the Mind, Body, and Spirit Expo to The Children's Hospital of Philadelphia to Bancorp, Inc.

Sarah Bernardi Carkner
Sarah Carkner Enterprises
www.sarahcarkner.com
info@sarahcarkner.com
610-220-0393

My Peace, My Place, My Joy!

Sheila Gibson Helme

"How many times have I told you the coffee cup handles should be at four o'clock and the knife blades must be turned toward the plates?" I screamed at Neva, my best waitress. "We've got three hundred people coming for cocktails and dinner tonight and these tables are set all wrong!"

"Sheila," someone behind me said. I spun around, expecting to see our client with an issue that needed attention. No one was there. I turned back and saw Neva beginning to tear up and look confused.

Again I heard the voice. "Sheila, you don't belong here—weren't you going to do something meaningful with your life?" The voice was strong and clear, and shook me to my bones.

"Are you okay?" Neva asked.

"No, I'm not," I said. "I'm so sorry. Can you handle this group through set-up and cocktail time and I'll be back before dinner service?"

"Sure...you look like you've seen a ghost."

"No...I didn't see a thing..."

My mind raced as I turned toward the elevator. *Who the hell was that? Great, now I'm hearing voices! Well, just one voice, but still...I'm way too stressed—too many hours, too little sleep, too much coffee in the morning, too much booze at night, and too many cigarettes in between. Is this what a nervous breakdown feels like?*

By the time I reached my office I held a cocktail in one hand and an unlit cigarette in the other. *I need to get it together—I have three hundred people upstairs for a banquet —my staff needs me.* I sat down, closed my eyes, and felt every cell of my body vibrating.

I put down the cocktail and cigarette and began to cry. *Where do I belong if not here? I thought I was doing pretty well with no college degree!* After a car accident and painful back injury I had to drop out, and couldn't afford to return. When able to work again I did what I knew—waiting tables. I moved on to bartending, bar managing, and up to assistant director of catering for a busy, somewhat classy hotel. I supervised a staff of thirty people. They called me the 007 of banquets for my ability to stay cool in every crisis.

So what's wrong with this? I wondered. Well, yelling at my best waitress for one. That's not like me. I didn't yell when I found her smoking pot in a car with the kitchen staff. I addressed it as I always do—calmly and in private.

Sometimes I rage inside, but I'm always calm and in control on the surface, I thought. Who am I kidding? I'm always raging inside! I hate my job, and I'm so out of control! I'm twenty-eight, a hundred pounds overweight, work sixty hours a week, stressed to the max, alone, lonely, sad, mad, and hearing a voice which has vanished...where are you now, with your advice? What do I do now?

Maybe God spoke to me...really Sheila, GOD? Do you think God has time for this craziness? Maybe it's my guardian angel, or my grandfather...I still miss him. I saw him recently in a dream. He was sitting on my bed, telling me everything was going to be fine. It felt so real—maybe he's talking to me...

OK, I'm ready to listen. What should I be doing with my life? Should I study massage therapy? I had thought of it often...it was the key to my healing after the car accident. I'd have to change my whole life, relocate, and find another job. Do you think I could do that? Do I think I could do that? Where are you now? Can you help me now, please?

Peace washed over me, deep abiding peace...quiet and calm. It didn't last long, a few moments maybe, but enough to give me a taste of what could be. In those few moments my awareness shifted to other times in my life when a calm and reassuring presence had filled me, quieted me, protected me, and I knew I was not alone.

Images began to flash through my mind. For as long as I could remember I'd been aware of someone—*something*— that showed up in times of fear and confusion. I had no name for it, just a deep awareness of this presence in my life. Suddenly, I realized I'd felt separated from this presence for years. Something had been missing, and now I knew what it was. I understood that this presence was the source of the voice I had heard.

The phone rang—they needed me upstairs. *Good, I need to get back to work and think about this later—much later!* For the next few days I could think of little else.

A Brave New World

With massage on my mind, I decided to check out a healing center near my home. I discovered they not only offered massage, they also taught a massage therapy certification course in that very building. Classes were held at night and I learned there was a lot of independent study involved, so I convinced management at the hotel to switch me to a daytime bartending job. I borrowed money for school and enrolled. One year later, I quit my job and jumped into massage therapy full-time.

I stood on the threshold of a whole new life, a new way of being in the world. I loved my work and connecting with people on a deeper level. I knew I was making a difference in people's lives. Still, I had many hurdles to overcome. Each step in the direction of my dream was accompanied by fear that threatened to hold me back.

As I worked with a variety of clients and their individual needs, I began to have an awareness of something beyond the physical substance of muscle, bone, and sinew. Life-force energy, which I perceive as light, or vibration, was the new piece of the puzzle. I started studying energy healing with a passion, and shared it with my clients. My own spiritual growth seemed to go hand in hand with my energy awareness.

In time I realized the voice I heard that day—the guiding guardian presence—was my higher self, an ever present part of me, a divine spark of light from God that each of us carries. When I stopped listening to the wisdom of my higher self, it spoke to me in a voice I could neither ignore nor deny. When I listened, the pieces of the puzzle began to fall into place and my life became a joyous adventure.

Guided on a path to healing the emotional wounds of my childhood, for years I was led to many different therapies, healers, and teachers. My creative side blossomed anew, and joys of my childhood returned as I wrote poetry, painted, and appreciated my deep connection with nature. I learned to meditate and fed my soul with divine light.

As I released the pain carried in my heart and soul, my body began to heal as well. I quit smoking during massage school and lost a hundred pounds the following year. Although still challenged by weight issues, I've never returned to that level of imbalance. Feeding my body with fresh, healthy food and joyful movement, I learned to respect it as a vehicle for love, light, healing, and joy.

The more I aligned my life with my heart, soul, and higher self, the more my experience of life expanded. A world filled with unexpected gifts and surprises resulted. An opportunity to work with a local hospice creating a Touch-Therapies program allowed me to share the work I cherish with the terminally ill and educate the medical professionals who care for them.

Wonderful people crossed my path in unexpected ways and shared their wisdom and light with me. Doors opened and opportunities were manifest to share my light through poetry and guided meditation projects. Travel to sacred places in Ireland and Egypt brought me deeper insights.

A Change of Plans

One day when I was forty-three I received an ordinary phone call that changed my life forever.

"Sheila Beth, can you join me downtown for happy hour tonight?" asked my friend Annie.

"No thanks, I have two more clients this afternoon and then, you know, I like to curl up on the couch with a movie and Vinny."

"Come on, it's a bank party—drinks are on my boss!" she implored. Annie called every Friday and each time I declined in favor of a video at home with my beloved coonhound.

"OK, but if you change your mind, we'll be at the Ritz."

Shortly after hanging up I received two more phone calls. Both of my clients cancelled with last minute emergencies. *Now what?* I thought. *You should go,* my inner voice urged. *Why not?* I agreed. *What could happen?*

"Vinny, you're on your own tonight," I said as I walked out the door.

That night I met Skip—my partner, lover, husband, and best friend. His plans had changed that evening, too. His two girls, Claire and Leah, had an event at church, so he'd decided to end his week meeting a friend for a drink.

His friend turned out to be Jim, a guy I'd known for years. On our wedding day a year later, Jim presented us with a photo taken months before our meeting. In the picture Skip was in the foreground and I was behind him at a concert we'd both attended separately with a large group of friends. Our paths had crossed for years—in grocery stores, restaurants, at events, and parties—but we'd never met!

That Friday—when we least expected it—we stood face to face with our future and smiled in recognition. My life with Skip—with our family—is the home I had longed for, body and soul. Of course, Vinny fell in love with Skip, too!

Now, after twenty-seven years of listening, I feel the divine presence of my higher self as close as my breath. Its gifts of awareness and joy are woven daily into the fabric of my being. My heart and hands are filled with its presence as I work with my clients, and help them nurture and understand their own light.

I feel it in my connection to the earth. It fuels the fire of my creativity. It's the core of the courage I need to act on my ideas and dreams, and the love that infuses each action. It's my voice when I share my truth, and the intuition that guides me. Most of all, it's my connection to the divine, to Mother-Father-God, the source of all that is. It's my peace, my place, my joy.

ABOUT THE AUTHOR: Sheila Gibson Helme works with a wide variety of clients providing Quantum-Touch, Reiki, Cranial Sacral and Massage Therapy to serve them in their physical and spiritual healing. The name of her business, Lightgarden Healing Arts expresses her desire to aid each and every client in knowing, nurturing and growing the light within. The focus of her work has recently expanded with the creation of Lightgarden Meditations, a CD to guide the listener to the discovery of the joy and gratitude that is as close as our breath. Sheila is a poet and a passionate advocate for creative expression as healing.

Sheila Gibson Helme, RMT, TRM, CQTP
www.lightgardenhealingarts.com
www.cdbaby.com/cd/sheilagibsonhelme
sheila@lightgardenhealingarts.com
719-632-4840

Keep The Faith

Maria Mantovano

"Maria, I don't think *any* color will help me, but go ahead and try it!" Rosetta agreed pessimistically. My heart sank as I realized her lack of innate empowerment and I was instantly motivated by an inner desire to make her feel good about herself.

Rosetta visited me weekly, and this week I'd offered her a color change before I began to style her hair. With her permission I created a violet/red hair color that I knew would compliment her beautiful green eyes and light skin. When I finished she looked at herself in the mirror and her eyes filled with tears.

"Oh my God—thank you!" she gushed. Her metamorphosis was incredible. It brought out the best in her features, and she couldn't stop thanking me. The look in her eyes remains with me to this day.

My desire to bring out the best in everyone made going into the beauty industry a natural choice for me. When behind the chair my clients became more than just clients—they were humans, people who had lives, individuals dealing with the complexities of life.

I often *felt* their story when they came to see me, and my gift was making them feel and look better than when they first arrived.

The Power of Faith

Born with the gifts of empathy, insight, and intuition, I often saw and knew things on a deeper level than most. Always conscious of a higher self, I evaluated situations and people more on an emotional level than an intellectual one.

Brought up in a home where my parents divorced when I was almost eleven, I remember my mother sitting there crying, filled with doubt and fear, not knowing her future. Out of necessity, I took over as caretaker for my mother, two sisters, and grandparents.

Even at such a tender age I viewed things with a mature outlook and shouldered great responsibility.

Happy that, with their divorce, there was finally peace in the house—no more fights, no more tears—I knew I didn't want to be around negative, emotional, and critical people. I wanted better. I knew I had a purpose, though I didn't know what that was exactly, and I prayed daily and spoke to God as if he was standing right next to me. I felt scared and without an answer, God became my parent. Always I knew with true confidence that if I called out to him, the saints, or the angels, I was heard and there'd be a resolution to my request.

Eventually both my mother and father moved down different paths, and I became a child raising children. My mom lived in the Bronx with her new husband, and my dad—well, he had many addresses. My father really had no interest in taking care of his three daughters and went his own way.

Easily hurt, I learned quickly I had only myself. I remember sitting and praying and writing all my desires and concerns early on, and since then, I've continued to seek knowledge through prayer. The responsibility of raising my sisters and tending to my grandparents' needs was overwhelming sometimes, and I prayed to God I made the right decisions when my mother wasn't there. I never wanted to fall short of doing the right thing and letting anyone down.

I took them to doctors, food-shopped, cooked, and helped them on a daily basis. I never regretted a moment and always felt secure and purposeful when taking care of my sisters and grandparents. Was I hurt? Can abandonment issues surface in your life because of rejection from a parent? It was painful not having my father attend any functions that were milestones growing up, but along the way I brushed off and buried a lot of emotions.

What hurt more than my parents' abandonment was when my friend Abbey's mother told her we could no longer be friends because I "came from a divorced home." That day I learned the meaning of ignorance. But even in my darkest days I always kept my faith. I felt purposeful and sensed goodness in all types of people—even though goodness was not part of my daily life. I was blessed to know at an early age that people were driven for different reasons but that we are all the same—all from the same source, just perceived differently by our words and actions.

Beauty School Dropout—*Not!*

I had several careers within the beauty industry, including owning a barbershop, working for Paul Mitchell and Empire. I soon realized my calling was much more than beauty. Driven by my strong inner desire to make everyone feel good, no matter their physical appearance, I truly believe everyone is beautiful. My emotional attachment to so many in such a special way enhances my ability to assist others with their beauty needs.

I progressed into teaching to benefit my students by sharing what I knew, and it was when I became a student counselor at a beauty/cosmetics school in Manhattan that I really began to feel connected on an even deeper level. Able to interact with each student and get to know who they were and what they wanted—their dreams and desires, their hearts, what path they wanted to pursue—I saw each of them as special and wanted to assist in their success.

I saw many students who struggled on a daily basis just to get to school. They came from single-parent homes, had daycare issues—some even lived in shelters. Life was hard for them, but they were there trying to make it better. I empathized with those students who felt lost and didn't have a parent there to cheer them on. My heart reached out to them and I encouraged them to keep moving and better themselves with a career that was theirs. I often told them their talent was right in their hands and no one could take it from them. They knew I had compassion and I taught them to look at someone's features and enhance what was already there—that it was so much a part of our job.

I showed these students their points of view in the eyes of someone else—I wanted them to look in the mirror and see the beautiful beings they truly are. I uplifted their spirits and shared knowledge that I believe was given to me on a spiritual level. I felt their pain and they knew I meant what I said even though I was straightforward that the information I received was from a higher source.

Part of me wanted to heal the pain I felt in so many, and part of me discovered why I was in this business—I was able to get them to drop their resistance and open up when no one else could. One particular graduate came to me when I was promoted into student services and career planning. Latoya entered my office one day, head down, and asked if I could help her. Immediately I felt her pain and my eyes filled with tears.

"Of course I can," I replied "What do you need?"

She began to cry. She told me she was a graduate of the school who'd gone through some hard times, lost everything, and was living in a shelter. Now she wanted to obtain her license but didn't have the books or other necessary tools she needed to proceed with the testing.

"Ok, give me a few days, and come back—and make sure you bring a backpack," I told her.

Her eyes showed a glimmer of hope as she agreed to return. Immediately I contacted my academic director to see if I could assist Latoya with the books and reading materials she needed for her test. Then I collected my own extra copies of the books and other materials she'd need.

I'll never forget Latoya's humbleness when she returned with her backpack and I filled it with everything to help her succeed in her life. We hugged and cried and I wished her a life full of success. I wanted her to know she wasn't alone, and that in life doors can open even when they seem to be closed. I told her to keep faith and to live life to the fullest...

Higher Ground

I know my path in this life is to assist people to feel secure and to let them know I'm their cheerleader. I want to help them look and feel their best—physically, mentally and emotionally—and to understand that inside each of us is *our inner being.* To me, this is God, and we are never really alone. All we have to do is be still and listen, for we all have the power to reach into ourselves and obtain the answers. God communicates in many wondrous ways, whether through a feeling, an intuitive sense of knowing, or signs that sometimes we ignore.

My mission in life is to mentor and share my life experience— failure and success, hurt and happiness, loneliness and fulfillment, pain into joy. When I coach students I emphasize how big a role we play in making someone's day by our touch, our words, or just by being there to listen. I tell them that those of us who help others come into their own sense of beauty are true healers.

I build my students' confidence and watch them grow, and I grow, too—emotionally and intellectually—but most of all spiritually. Able to see natural talent versus the students who struggle to just get it, my eyes and heart are open to all and I want to help.

I've learned many things in life, including that I still want to grow spiritually. I research matters of ascending to a higher spiritual level continually, and seek ultimate knowledge of who and what I can be to create a path of non-resistance and peace. I look to attract like minds of conscious beings and to be one with God and my higher spirit.

I am now working on my book to mentor cosmetology students and graduates about career placement and opportunities to help empower each individual on their journey toward personal dreams and goals. My joy lies with coaching anyone who's ever felt sad, lonely, or defeated, and showing them how they can rebuild themselves from the inside out. In the process, I give them tips on creating a new look, a makeover, and healing, and tell them "go forward, the power is in *your hands* to create and empower" others!

I love what I do and am fully in gratitude for the things that happened in my life, and for the person I am today! I want to love and be loved and share my journey through the prayers I write and my own evolution. I want to serve the community and give back. Life is so much more than what we make it, as long as we keep the faith...

ABOUT THE AUTHOR: A beauty industry professional, Maria Mantovano is a sought after teacher, mentor, and spiritual guide who educates and assists others with their beauty needs and concerns. Maria's belief that everyone is beautiful led her to mentor beauty school students about the *real* role they play in their clients' lives—to enhance clients' outer beauty to best match their inner beauty, to accentuate their positives, and to enhance their self-esteem. Currently working on a book for future professionals now entering the beauty industry, empathic and compassionate Maria shares her expertise about how to help people look and feel their best always.

Maria Mantovano
Beauty Expert
mariamantovanobeautyexpert@gmail.com
609-432-0309

For Love of Family ~ and Chocolate!

Susan Hordych

There were two rules growing up in my family: Dinner is at five-thirty and you *will* be home; and you will *not* be late! Dinner time was family time. You were not allowed to leave the table because someone knocked on the door or called to see if you could come out to play.

Every night Dad sat at his spot at the head of the table, and told stories about his own experiences growing up. He wanted to ensure his four children were schooled in life and the realities that accompany it. Taught at an early age the importance of family, I understood that helping one another and knowing we'd each encounter our own obstacles and face our own situations, was part of life. Family, without judgment, will do whatever needs to be done to help!

Part of mom and dad's "school of life" was to instill in their children the value of a dollar, and the hard work required to earn that dollar. I, being the eldest, was the first to be taught that lesson. I obtained my first job at eleven—a paper route—for which you needed to be twelve, but a birth certificate was not required. The paper's sections were dropped off at my house every morning, and I'd assemble the paper for delivery after school, load the baskets on my ten-speed bicycle, and deliver to those on my route. After-school programs were an option *only* after discussing the change in delivery time with all my customers.

My ten-speed served me well as I took on an additional job as a chambermaid in Seaside Heights, N.J., for the summer season. I rode my bike over the bridge from my house in Toms River rain or shine, every day! Sometimes I was lucky and received a ride, but my parents both worked and told me when I got the job it was my responsibility to get to work on time.

One crisp autumn morning in the fall of 1982 I hopped on my trusty ten-speed and peddled down the street to my new job—a candy store had opened recently and the candy season was just beginning. Little did I know this new job would affect the rest of my life on so many different levels. Fifteen and a freshman in high school, I was introduced to what would one day become my passion—chocolate!

My first day, two days before Thanksgiving, was overwhelming but enjoyable. That year I learned basic day-to-day operations, the proper temperature for melting chocolate, and how to make hollow and solid molds. I dipped my first strawberry, and soon developed a talent for and love of dipping.

At first I didn't have the knack and didn't think I ever would. With no digital thermostats on the pots then, I didn't know exactly when the temperature was right for dipping. I'd put some chocolate on a lollipop stick, press it against my lip to gauge the temperature, and—though it took some time—finally succeeded in dipping a perfect strawberry with a swirl on top!

My senior year in high school I took a full-time job at Household Finance. I'd taken business courses and appeared to be headed in the direction of a banking career. After graduation, I continued to work seasonally in the candy store and covered the store whenever the owners were away.

How Sweet It Is!

I met my husband Stan while the owners were on vacation and I was taking care of the store. He was house-sitting and the store was attached.

"Watch the house, not the employee," he'd been told. Fearless, he invited me for dinner after work one night and the rest is history! I was twenty-one at the time and knew right away he was a keeper since he was a really good cook!

We married and moved from Toms River to north Jersey, since Stan worked at the main chocolate store in Paramus after getting laid off from his construction job. There he did the cooking and preparing of the candies for the dippers. I realized after the birth of our daughter, Cassandra, how much I missed my family and their unending support. Shortly after returning to work full time I was laid off from my job, and found employment at the candy store for the Easter holiday. We knew Stan would be unemployed for the summer, so when he said "pack your bags, we're going home," we did just that.

The winter of 1992 brought along Daniel. Soon enough, Stan and I had four kids and full-time jobs. He found side work too, while I worked nights and weekends at a retail store as we struggled to get by. Although dipping berries seemed like a faded memory it was still something I continued doing, only now in my own kitchen. I always made Easter candy for our kids, along with platters for my mom to gift to her clients at holiday time.

One day I made some extra goodies and Stan brought them to work and sold them all. I enjoyed the creative outlet, and with the extra money I bought the kids a swing set. I felt a deep sense of pride and accomplishment, exactly what my parents had strived so hard to teach me! From that moment on I knew that somehow, some way, I'd own my own candy store...

Soon I found employment as an office manager for a local business and Stan worked for K. Hovnanian. My parents wanted to sell their house—the one in which I'd grown up—and approached us about purchasing it. We jumped at the offer, and life seemed to fall in to place nicely. Soon after our move, however, I was laid off and spent the summer at home with the kids.

I knew my reality needed two full-time incomes, and that if we wanted anything we both had to work. Finding a job within the salary range and proximity of my prior employment proved difficult. I concluded I'd have to commute, and after several interviews landed a job as an office manager for a contractor in Middletown. We'd always lived within a few miles from where I worked and now commuting added a whole new obstacle. Stan already commuted and what site he was working at determined when he got home. What used to be my normal routine no longer was normal—with the kids' new schedules for school everything seemed to change in such a short period of time...

A Woman Who Wants Her Chocolate

The contractor I worked for did business with the owner of the Village Mall, and tried to convince us to open a shop there. Together we knew the front and back ends of the chocolate making business, so we thought a candy store was perfect. We talked—knowing the hours and dedication it would take to make it work and how much would be at stake if it didn't prove successful—and decided to approach the owners of the candy store where we'd both learned the trade to see if they'd allow us to franchise.

They agreed—now we needed financing! The bank refused us a loan, and Stan was against a lien on our home, so we pulled out every credit card we had in hopes of making our dream a reality. Petrified, we knew if it didn't succeed we had no idea how we'd pay our credit card bills. No stranger to hard work—I liked it, had always done it, and working seven days a week didn't bother me—I continued working for the contractor while I setup and stocked the store on my lunch hours. Watching my own candy shop come to life was magical!

Up and running, our credit cards maxed, Stan agreed to a loan on his 401(k) to consolidate the payments and take off some of the pressure. We finally got our finances in order—as in order as they could be for two people in debt up to their eyeballs—when we ran into the next hurdle. I was shocked to find out one day at work that the landlord had rented our storefront to another client! He offered us a different space, but it was a completely empty shell—no walls, floors, or ceiling! We'd have to build everything from the ground up, and were supposed to open in five weeks!

Terrified of telling Stan, I worried endlessly until finally I blurted it out that night. The result was one of the biggest fights we'd ever had. He wanted to forget the whole thing, just walk away, but I couldn't give up my dream. We'd reached the point where a decision had to be made—either I was going to let the business go or become a full-time chocolatier. After some cool down time, we agreed to proceed.

I threw myself into the store with a new vigor. It was really sink or swim now, because I no longer had a full-time job and the credit cards were not paid off yet. How I loved working in my own store! Aside from being with my family, I was happiest making candy. I never got sick of going to work; it wasn't a job I'd go to everyday and do the same thing. I worked in the front, the back, made baskets, did whatever I wanted...I still have such creative freedom at work—put me in the store, let me make chocolate and create gift baskets—I love it!

"All You Need is Love—But a Little Chocolate Now and Then Doesn't Hurt!" ~ Charles M. Schulz

Five years later Suzi's Sweet Shoppe became an independent store and I've never looked back! My experience as an office manager prepared me for the day-to-day responsibilities of running the business and proved invaluable. It's not all just sitting at the dipping pot!

Today we offer much more than when we could as a franchised business. We're family-owned and operated—you get an email or call from me, not a computer generated one! I pride myself on personalized customer service and the fact that our candy is made fresh daily—it doesn't sit on a shelf for six months! I listen to my customers' concerns and suggestions, and can be as creative as I see fit.

Stan and I make day trips to other states for site inspection of other candy establishments and look for new ideas. We attend large candy shows in other states, too, and seminars and workshops in an effort to constantly evolve and improve what we offer. I continue to experiment with new chocolate delights, and use my family as test subjects. Dad has the final say on anything marshmallow, while Mom provides input on creams and peanut butter. My sisters and brother comment on everything!

Through it all, the constant support and encouragement of my family was key. I continue to pass on to my children the love of family—and chocolate!

ABOUT THE AUTHOR: Susan Hordych and her husband, Stan are proud owners of a confectionery haven known as Suzi's Sweet Shoppe. Even as a teenager, she was passionate about candy, so she built her candy coated dream come true while starting and raising a family. Susan is active in many local organizations and travels the country with her husband to various expositions, always looking for something new. In many ways, Susan has taken candy to a new level, and the world is her chocolate covered strawberry—a favorite among patrons. Susan plans to continue building on her chocolate dreams working alongside family and surrounded by love.

Susan Hordych
Suzi's Sweet Shoppe
www.SuziSweetShoppe.com
Suzi@SuziSweetShoppe.com
732-796-0115

The Joys of Boot Camp!

Sue Meredith

Every Monday morning I'd wake up, ready myself for work, and start driving into town. The closer I got to my office the more I'd feel my face become hot and flushed—my blood pressure definitely was up! Suddenly I'd feel a panic attack coming on, burst into tears, and cry all the way to work.

I hate going to that office! I'd think as I drove to work those mornings. *Here I am again, just like every other Monday, stressed out already and the week hasn't even begun!*

In truth, this Monday morning anxiety set in on Sunday night as my mood turned horrific and my anxiety level increased drastically—so much so that no one wanted to be around me. Cranky, miserable, and irritable, friends and family would say to me "why don't you go to the doctor for some medication to fix that?"

My response was always the same: "You have to fix the situation, not mask it with drugs, because you'll still be in the same predicament—only with drugs!" I hated feeling this way and not being able to make my family happy. This only happened during my work week, of course...

Everything seemed like a blur during those years due to stress. My weekends were fabulous—I'd relax with my husband and son and have fun. It was my escape—time when I'd hide from the real world, shut off my phone, and try to disappear from my work environment totally. But on Sunday night, reality would set in again and I'd feel my chest tighten, my anxiety level skyrocket, and my blood pressure begin to get out of control.

I'd helped run the family business for more than twenty years, but hated going to that office! I thanked my parents silently every day for the opportunity they gave me, and I learned a lot during the process, but the stress and burnout proved to be too much for me! I listened to customers call in every day and complain—they were hot, or refrigeration was down again. Sure, they were happy when we arrived on the scene and got them up and running again the same day. Then they'd receive the bill!

Of course, when you own your own business you have issues concerning staff, co-workers, customers, and vendors. It took several years before I began to experience chest pains and anxiety attacks, but when this kind of stress persisted throughout the day and I began to blow up at meetings, I knew I had to quit. I understood also that I had to tell my parents—they helped to make me successful and who I am today, but I just couldn't do it anymore!

I had to leave for my sanity and health, and I decided to make a change before I experienced serious health issues, wound up in the hospital, or lost my family entirely. The hardest part was thinking about telling them I was done because I feared disappointing them, especially my brother, who was also involved in the business.

The War Zone

The first thing I realized was that I'd lost all of my social skills sitting in an office all day talking only to people on the phone—and often these were not the most pleasant conversations! I knew when I made my move I'd have to learn to interact with people face-to-face again, but that this challenge would be well worth it for the sake of my happiness.

I decided to go back to school part-time, before I talked to my family about leaving the business, and learn to do what I loved most—personal health and fitness training. I spent my weekends at the local college getting my certification, and worked long nights at the gym to get even more experience, though I've always worked out and tried to stay fit. Nobody at my office knew I was doing this—I wasn't going to let anyone put me down or try to stop me with negative feedback. This was my out—someday.

Soon I managed to become a certified boot camp instructor, and opened my first location. I began my days at four a.m., and my first class started at five-thirty a.m. This gave me just enough time to finish class, get to my office before anyone else arrived, and prepare for another dreadfully long day of listening to everyone complain.

I'd leave at five p.m. and head back to the gym for personal training. When I arrived home about seven p.m., I'd cook dinner, clean the house, and wash laundry with the help of my husband and son, and head off to bed around eleven p.m. This made for long days, but Darryl and Garrett were behind me one hundred percent.

The day of our annual company meeting arrived—another two hours of my life I dreaded every year because you never knew what was going to happen. Maybe I stressed myself out for no reason, but this was the meeting that broke me down every year. On a dark, hot, muggy night in 2010, the meeting started off calmly enough but slowly began to escalate as partners raised their voices.

I walked quietly over to my desk, and pulled out a binder that weighed about fifteen pounds, contained 2,000+ pages, and was filled with twenty years of specifics about what I did to run the company. The book included screen shots and detailed instructions on everything from turning on the lights in the office in the morning to handling employees, customers, vendors, banking, and accounting, up to and including locking the door at night. It had taken me several years to write this book.

I moved to the middle of the room where everyone could see me and *slammed* the book on the floor.

"Enough!" I yelled. Immediately silence filled the room. "I can't take this anymore! I'm sick of it—being stressed out and miserable! Trying to make everyone else happy *sucks* and it's making me even *more* miserable! *I can't do this anymore, I'm through!"*

Everyone stared at me and the meeting pretty much ended there. After the other company members left the office I had a long talk with my parents and brother. Relieved when they said they completely understood and it would be ok—things would work out—I revealed how worried I'd been about disappointing them if I left after running the business for twenty years. I wanted my parents to be able to retire and enjoy life without having to work themselves to death. I didn't think my dad should have to be working on rooftops fixing air conditioners in 100-degree heat at age sixty-five. After all, he'd worked on rooftops 24/7 for forty years!

The process of leaving the company dragged on for a couple more years, and then we received a purchase offer. Since all of the partners were ready to move on to new ventures, this benefitted everyone. But it took until April 2012 to conclude the whole process. I stayed on with the new owners another month to smooth the transition, and to introduce customers and vendors to the new owners.

Free At Last...

May 18, 2012 is a day I'll never forget—my last day of working at a desk! Woo Hoo, was I happy! Despite my euphoria, though, it was scary to venture out on my own and step outside of my box. I got the evil eye and cold shoulder all day at work, but not from my parents who were now out enjoying themselves. My brother had decided to leave the new company in search of something new, too. The only thing I received at the end of the day was a "good bye." As perturbing as that seemed at first, upon reflection I realized I was free! *I'm in control of my own destiny!* I thought. *No one can drag me down...*

Now I smile and laugh all the time. I act silly and don't care who notices. I no longer have nightmares about work, my energy's increased, and I haven't had one chest pain! My husband says I'm a totally different person—in a good way!

Currently I own two boot camp locations where my ladies work out, have fun, and support each other. Their confidence levels soar by the time they finish their four-week sessions, and they make new friends as well. I'm working on my master trainer certification to further my education and help my clients succeed, and to become a certified personal fitness chef.

I love concocting healthy recipes from everyday items in the refrigerator. My goal is to write a cookbook, and so far my recipes have been terrific! My family always jokingly asks "aren't you going to take a picture of your plate?" When I do, it turns into a masterpiece for my new book! The fun part is taking pictures at each step of the process, which is only a little less enjoyable than tasting my new recipes!

The biggest challenge I've faced since running my own business full-time is keeping my house clean and doing all of the laundry. I do have help from rest of the family and I thank Darryl and Garrett from the bottom of my heart for being so supportive during this transition period. The way I look at it—anything that doesn't get done will be there tomorrow, and it's not the end of the world...it will get done eventually.

I'm grateful also to my parents and my brother for their unswerving allegiance during this whole transitional experience. Also, in the process of my leaving one career for another, my husband bravely decided to take up the challenge of leaving behind a boss to become involved with my new business venture. He's studying for his personal trainer certification and we have plans to expand our knowledge together and help others learn the benefits of exercise and healthy living.

In January 2013 I put together a team of boot campers, spouses, and friends to compete in my first ever mud run obstacle course. A huge success, we all survived and had a blast—proof positive that I can do anything to which I put my mind! I am so glad I decided to step outside my box and was brave enough to pursue my dream! Calm and relaxed, now I enjoy going to work every day, free from the stress and strain of my former career. By being myself, I'm satisfied and happy knowing I can help make someone else's day, too. It wasn't easy moving out of the tensions of my former career and into the joys of boot camp, but it was worth every minute!

ABOUT THE AUTHOR: Coach, personal trainer, and motivator Sue Meredith invites you to join her on a fun-filled healthy journey to learn how to make healthy food choices and exercise a fun part of your day, every day. Founder of Fort Myers/Cape Coral Adventure Boot Camp for women, Sue's involvement in personal fitness began early in life when she worked out with her three older brothers. Since then, she's studied weight training and personal development, researched many areas of fitness, and now realizes her dream to help others experience the benefits of a well-rounded and healthy lifestyle.

Sue Meredith
Susan Meredith Fitness Enterprises
www.SueMeredith.com
getfit@fortmyersadventurebootcamp.com
239-220-2269

Calling All Angels!

AmondaRose Igoe

When I found myself on my knees in my office crying profusely, it became crystal clear that something needed to change, and it needed to change *now*. Completely out of control, I knew only an extremely quick and effective solution could get me out of this mess!

When it came to living a balanced life, I'd hit my personal rock bottom. I found myself crying every day from sheer exhaustion. Working non-stop, I hadn't taken a day off in a very long time. My career mentors—the people I looked up to in my business—were telling me to work even harder and devote even more hours to achieve the level of success I desired.

At the time I didn't realize I was allowing other people to dictate how I ran my life and my business. I went from a basically happy person to an emotional and overworked wreck. I spiraled out of control trying to achieve my business vision and didn't know how to change my totally crazy workaholic behavior. This was *not* how I envisioned my life as an entrepreneur!

As I knelt on my office floor, I did the only thing I knew how to do—pray for an answer. I'd tried to change my out of balance life and out of control behavior on my own and nothing I did worked. It became obvious at that moment that I needed assistance to achieve my desired state of balance. At the least, I would certainly have to do some things differently. I didn't know where to begin. Out of desperation, I looked for answers from a higher source....

From Heaven Above

Within a few days of my request for spiritual intervention, a friend who didn't know what was happening shared with me that she learned how to change her life by increasing the divine help she was getting from above. Immediately, I wanted to know more.

Robin asked if I'd ever thought about hiring angels to help me create the life I desired. She'd just read a book called "Hiring the Heavens" by Jean Slatter that spoke of the many "unemployed angels" with specific talents and skills ready and willing to help those of us here on Earth. I simply needed to ask for their help, she explained.

"It's very simple," Robin told me. "For example, if you need computer help, you simply request an angel with computer skills to handle the challenge! If you misplace a ring, hire a spiritual detective angel to ensure that you find it."

Wow, it sounded so simple! I realized quickly I needed to hire my angels and tell them what I wanted. I could use them for one task, to put together a specific business-building team, or to handle family obligations. *Well,* I thought, *at this point in my life I've got nothing to lose—I might as well give it a try!*

Though I considered myself a spiritual person, I'd never actively or consistently sought out the help of angels. At the time, I believed in the existence of angels—*kind of*—so I figured I had nothing to lose. Immediately I began to hire away, and the results astounded me! For example, my dear friend Carol was getting married outdoors in the California hills, surrounded by beautiful red oak trees. The weather forecaster had predicted a full day of rain, and indeed there was a torrential downpour outside.

I couldn't let this happen to Carol, so I said "I need a Perfect Weather Angel right now to clear the rain and bring out the sun! Carol deserves a beautiful wedding day!" Within five minutes of my request the rain stopped completely and the skies became crystal clear and a beautiful shade of light blue. Thanks to the angels, my dear friend had the most glorious outdoor wedding imaginable! At one point, just as she and her husband were saying their beautiful vows, we even saw the sun and the moon in the sky. From that moment on, I requested angelic help all the way through the next day—we never saw another drop of rain or a cloud in the sky!

My angels created much magic in my life as well. Since starting my own business in 2004, I'd carried the weight of the world on my shoulders. I believed the success of my business was determined by how hard I was willing to work and the amount of hours I was willing to put in. That often meant working sixty to seventy hours a week and taking very little time off. If I continued that way, I knew over time I'd risk my health and physical well being.

From the moment I hired my first angel onto my angelic business-building team, I no longer felt alone. Immediately, help seemed available to me 24/7, and no task or challenge proved too big to handle. Since then I've employed on my business-building team a "Prosperity and Abundance Creator," "Priceless Personal Assistant Angel," "Master Marketing Angel," "Positive People Plus Attitude Monitor Angel," and many more!

As a result, new business opportunities popped up in the most unexpected and miraculous of ways. People began to ask questions and make positive comments.

"I see your business photo and name everywhere," said one. "What are you doing?"

"How is your business growing so quickly?" queried others. Because the power of angels is meant to be shared (anyone can gain access to them), I was more than happy to explain how to hire angels to create incredible business growth to anyone open to this concept.

The Creation Of Joy

I'd lost my love for life quite some time ago and replaced it with the concept that hard work was more important. Now seriously out of balance, my angels enabled me to reconnect with my sheer joy for life. With them on my side, I no longer felt like I was completely disconnected from my feelings of joy. These angelic helpers simply required that I was willing to help them create what I like to call "magical, miraculous, and magnificent" results in my life.

Once I learned to ask for specific help, I began to see the angels' quickness and resourcefulness in my life. Implementing steps that I still utilize today, I opened my mind and my mouth to ask for specific help and didn't wait until I was desperate. I know now that angels are not limited by the timing of a request, nor does it matter how big or small the task—my angels have proven to me consistently that they are willing to help me anytime, anywhere, and in any way.

After I ask for help, I express gratitude. For me, real gratitude means celebrating the small changes that lead to abundant successes. Personally, I like to break out into a happy dance when I receive the spiritual support I've requested. When driving, I talk to my angels and love to give them spiritual high fives! Any time something wonderful happens in my life, I make sure to say, "Thank you, angels!"

Finally, I had to learn to have fun again and to let go in the process. That meant I had to stop trying to control everything and start looking for more ways to create joyous opportunities in my life. It became very apparent that the more fun I had in my life, the easier and quicker my angels were able to help me.

At times, when I'd begin to fall back into my old pattern of not asking for help and of trying to do everything on my own I'd call on my "Ease, Grace, and Fun Angel," a.k.a. "Grace," and yell out "Grace, I need your help! I'm doing it again! I don't know how to let go and have fun!" Each time I asked "Grace" to intervene, a new understanding and ease overcame me and eventually the overworked and out of balance person I used to be disappeared. As a result, my business thrives with a lot less effort on my part...

Counting My Blessings

The day my friend Robin told me about the angels was the day I discovered how to once again have *real* fun and experience *true* joy. My angels set my spirit soaring and allowed me to reach a new level of ease I never thought possible. Now I envision new possibilities that I could never have created on my own with only human effort. The opportunities before me are truly limitless. My angels know no restrictions—they support, help, and love me at all times. Whatever I need, my angels answer all requests and ensure that each and every outcome is in my highest and best interests.

Little did I know how simple it could be! Finding a permanent and continuous path to absolute joy and fun in my life was simply a matter of calling all angels...

ABOUT THE AUTHOR: AmondaRose Igoe is an Award Winning 6-Figure Speaking Expert and Best Selling Author. AmondaRose specializes in helping business owners attract more clients and income by showing them how to design, deliver and book speaking engagements. The power of what AmondaRose teaches has helped her clients from around the globe including North America, Germany, Switzerland, England and Australia. AmondaRose is the is the author of "Pain-Free Public Speaking", a contributing author in the number #1 Best Selling book series "Chicken Soup for the Soul" and was a featured expert on the FOX 4 Television Station.

AmondaRose Igoe
6-Figure Speaking Goddess & Award Winning Speaker
www.AmondaRose.com
AmondaRose@amondarose.com
(800) 610-9056

Laughing Into Infinite Bliss

Anne Timpany

Cotton-mouthed panic floods my body as I crumple into a heap of quivering tears. The thought of leaving the safety net of marriage to become a single mom petrifies me. Though I've jumped out of airplanes hundreds of times, this leap of faith terrifies me infinitely more than plummeting through ten thousand feet of thin air. Without the reassuring weight of a parachute on my back, I have only my heart, intuition, and laughter to support me and my one year-old son as I free-fall into this next chapter of life, and it feels insane.

And yet, I know that I have to do this. I've imprisoned myself for years within the walls of my comfort zone, slowly dying a little bit every day. My heart is gasping for the air of expansion, begging me to breathe in life itself by stepping into new territory.

And now—*wham.* I've slammed head-on into a tidal wave of terror, after promising my heart I would honor it and "follow my bliss," in the words of Joseph Campbell.

This is not what I imagined bliss to be. I had a vague concept of an airy-fairy peaceful state, far beyond happiness, whatever that might be, but never did I associate "bliss" with sweaty palms and choking sobs. *Am I frightened of dying, or am I really afraid to live?*

Follow Your Bliss

When I first set out to "follow my bliss" three months ago, the idea of bliss felt more blank and mysterious than anything else. Faced with the economic reality of making the shift from stay-at-home mom to working mom, I discovered a part of myself that would no longer settle for simply paying the bills. *There must be more to life than this, but...what?* Getting a job just for the paycheck felt mind-numbingly dull, not blissful—but what was the alternative? *Do what you love,* my heart whispered. But under stress, I found myself drawing a blank. *How can I make a living doing what I love, if I don't even know what I love?*

Little motivational sayings became my lifeline, as the right quotes continued to show up, day after day, as inspiration. "The journey of a thousand miles begins with a single step." *Thanks, Lao Tzu. I can take a single step, but in which direction?* Writing down every idea that came to mind, wondering what kind of work I might like to do, the breeze of inspiration fanned a single spark—a glowing ember that had smoldered deep within ever since I'd read an unusual magazine article the previous year.

They say you teach that which you need to learn most. No kidding. The article had interviewed people who gathered others together to laugh for no apparent reason. *Okay, that's just nuts,* I thought. And yet, in my gut I knew I wanted to do that—no, I *had* to do that. Some unknown force tugged at my soul, pulling me in the direction of this oddly intriguing practice called Laughter Yoga, planting a seed in my mind that wouldn't go away, no matter how far I tried to push it out of my mind. *Was this the first step in the direction of bliss?*

Facing The Dragon

I have to become a laughter leader. The thought lit up an inner fire of excitement and simultaneously filled me with deep dread, for it meant accepting the fact that I was even crazier than I thought.

I had no idea where this journey would lead, or even what being a laughter leader entailed. I had even less of an idea whether I could make any money doing this. But Lao Tzu had assured me that a single step was all that was needed, so I stepped into the unknown, following this tiny glimmer of a spark that pulled me in the direction of...laughing. For a living. *Ugh...I am insane,* a voice within me groaned. Yet another part of me lit up with delight to have a dream to chase, a whisper of bliss to follow.

Three months later, this whisper of bliss had become a shout, and thank God, because a new realization had flooded my mind with a deafening cacophony of terror. The day before I flew to Albuquerque for a week of training to become a Certified Laughter Yoga Teacher, I awakened with the clarity of knowing it was time to file for divorce. I'd been trying so hard—and we'd been trying together—but I was no longer the person he married, and the kind thing to do was to let it go.

Tears of relief streamed from my eyes—or were they tears of panic? The path—no, the single step in front of me—was clear, thank God, but scary as hell. I couldn't see where it led and my mind had imprinted the message of doom all over the blank spaces on the map: *Beyond Here There Be Dragons. Shit.*

It's one thing to follow this whisper of bliss from within the safe nest of marriage and a place to call home, I thought. *It's another thing altogether to leap off the rocky cliff, burn all my bridges, and stake everything upon a wispy thread of trust and a few quotes written by a Chinese guy more than two thousand years ago. Shit, shit, shit. What am I doing?*

I was about to spend a week laughing for no reason—an activity that historically would likely have had me committed to an insane asylum—and suddenly my sanity felt tenuous at best. My next chapter of life would be as a single mom, and rather than capitalizing on my master's degree to find a sensible job with a steady paycheck and benefits, my plan (if you could call it that) to support myself and my son was to start over from scratch by...laughing? I put my head in my hands and sighed.

Follow your bliss, and doors will open...

Wiping my tears, I took a deep breath and felt a new sensation in my gut—a strength and a confidence that I could do this. *I can handle whatever comes, and I am fine.*

The Voice Of Truth

I have never laughed so much in my life. My cheeks hurt, my sides ache, yet my whole body feels like it is glowing. Training to become a Laughter Yoga Teacher requires, as you might expect, a lot of laughing. And eye contact. What is it about eye contact? Looking into the eyes of another human and laughing together is the most intimate experience I've ever encountered. I don't even know these people, and yet they feel like dear friends I've known forever.

"My name is Anne Timpany. Hee-hee-hee." The group erupts into uproarious laughter.

"I'm from Idaho-ho-ho-ha-ha." Loud guffaws punctuate the chorus of giggles flowing from the forty-plus members of the class.

"I am a mom with a one-year-old son, and I'm planning to teach Laughter Yoga and see where it leads." We all laugh as though this is the funniest thing we've ever heard.

This is simultaneously the strangest and most profound experience I've ever had. Laughing about ordinary declarations of identity illuminates the clear knowing that none of this is true at all, and that I am none of those things, these labels. What I am is beyond words, and the only sound that comes close to adequately expressing the truth is the sound of laughter—the physical expression of divinity in human form.

The Joy Is In The Journey

After five days of laughing with my new family—this group of more than forty women and men from all over the world—I am in love. I am in love with every single one of them. I am in love with life. I am in love with love. I am glowing, beaming, alive. I can't stop laughing, even if my sides ache. I want to hug everyone, to twirl around dancing with every passerby, to gaze into the eyes of every human on this planet and share the gift of laughter so that they, too, may know their own divinity. Oh, this gift of laughter! It's the secret that's been hidden in plain sight all this time.

I dance my way to the car, eager to pick up my son and start this new chapter of life. The sun glints off my windshield, creating a cascade of shimmering lights in the film of tears that has filled my eyes. After laughing for a week straight, suddenly all I can do is cry. A cataclysmic explosion of love, joy, and ecstasy has erupted from somewhere deep within, and the energy—too vast to be contained within my physical body—has found an outlet in a massive torrent of tears. My body shakes with sobs of gratitude as I smile at the sudden realization: *I set out to follow my bliss, and instead, bliss has found me.*

I'm driving out of Albuquerque, but I sense that I'm departing from something bigger, leaving a familiar paradigm of reality behind. Laughing has cracked open an old protective shell around my heart, smashing the wall of fear into smithereens. Through tears of joy, I can see clearly now: I am free. I don't need to have a clue where I am going or what the future holds. Safe and secure on the wings of my laughter parachute, I don't need to know anything but the deep conviction that I will always have everything I need in each moment, and my heart will always guide me—one step at a time.

Follow your bliss.

The simplicity of it all makes me laugh once again, and I look out the window through half-crying and half-chuckling sniffles and tears. I must look like a wild-haired, tear-stained mess to the people in the passing cars. I probably look like I'm insane. Ha. I am insane, by all conventional standards. I have left the herd, jumped off the cliff, and burned the bridges, plunging into the abyss of the unknown and splashing into the pool of infinite bliss.

ABOUT THE AUTHOR: Following her whisper of bliss to live a laughing life, Anne Timpany discovered that combining laughter with conscious intention opens the door to a wellspring of endless creativity, intuitive wisdom, and infinite joy. Integrating her passions for laughter, neuroscience, quantum awareness, and the mind-body connection, Anne's local and international Embodying Joy retreats and seminars educate and inspire through the power of play. As a speaker, writer, coach, and perpetual student, Anne continues to explore and share innovative ways that we humans can rewire our brains to fulfill our highest potential, enjoy optimal health, and live harmoniously in joy.

Anne Timpany
Embodying Joy Coaching and Retreats
www.embodyingjoy.com
anne@embodyingjoy.com
208-716-2465

That Which Doesn't Bend Will Break

Karen Sullivan

I sat in my police car on Main Street one cold night in February 1987 looking for speeders when a grey Honda Accord whizzed by doing sixteen miles over the speed limit. I "lit 'em up," police lingo for activating the overhead lights, since they were moving fast enough to take a look at, and I was going west to grab my two a.m. Dunkin' Donuts coffee soon anyway.

The Honda driver noticed me following him and accelerated suddenly. There was virtually no traffic, only a few cars on the road, and the Honda shot past them as if blown out of a cannon. Safe to say the Honda now far exceeded the posted thirty mile-per-hour speed limit by quite a bit, making the other cars look like they were standing still on the wrong side of the road.

I followed him west, through a few bends and dips in the road, and after one of the dips I lost him. The next thing I saw was flying snow— it had snowed a night or two earlier and snow lay on the side of the road—and then I spied the Honda crashed into a tree. There were light poles down and pieces of the Honda everywhere.

I jumped out of the car and everything went into slow motion. I felt like I was running but couldn't get anywhere. My partner ran to the driver side of the car; I had my gun in the passenger's ear. A drip of blood came from his nose, his ear, and his mouth, just like you see on T.V. Two sixteen year-old boys had a few beers, took the car on a joyride, and hadn't wanted to get caught so they took off. Sadly, the sixteen year-old passenger died.

At that time I was on the force about a year and a half, and there was no such thing as critical incident stress debriefings or talking to someone about what happened. You just brushed yourself off, went home to sleep, and came back to work to answer any questions posed by the prosecutor's office. I drove home that morning, numb. Though I called a friend and told her what happened, I didn't feel anything. Throughout my twenty-five years on the job, the blue suit was the armor I wore to tough things out and not show emotion because it was weak. And being a female who showed emotion was even weaker still.

The Protector

Even as a kid, I was always a protector of people. Growing up in Bayonne, N.J., I had great parents who summered with us at the Jersey Shore. I remember my sister Michelle came in the house crying after a kid punched her. The next thing I knew, the police were at the front door looking for me because I'd beaten the hell out of him.

Around the same time, a kid pushed my cousin Lori under a wave in the ocean. I'm not sure if it was Lavallette or Ortley Beach, but I almost drowned the kid by holding his head under several waves so he got the message not to mess with her again. A true Jersey girl, I spent a lot of time at my Aunt Di and Uncle Hal's house in New Providence, where there just happened to be a bully across the street who found it necessary to pick on my cousin. After I hit him a few times with a tree branch he got the message, too.

In 1984 I decided it was time to use this "protection" power that was second nature to me on a grander scale. Hired by the Chatham Borough Police Department, now I got to "protect and serve" as a career!

A woman in law enforcement, and the only one in the department, I figured I had to have thick skin so as not to be considered a wuss or a "girl." After all, people don't call the cops to come to the barbeque; they call the cops when the barbeque blows up! I could flip a switch, I could shut off my emotions and not deal with the sad or upsetting things that happened during the course of my career.

Most of the time, my ability to turn off emotionally made me crazy effective as a boss. The calls would come at three a.m., the blue suit would go on, and the emotions would go off. I hadn't felt anything when I found out the kid in the speeding Honda had died. I witnessed many "blow ups" over the years, and my modus operandi was to flip the switch.

Being tough could take different forms though, and didn't mean I ignored my intuition. Like the time my partner and I answered a domestic violence call at the home of a couple where the wife had smashed the windshield of her husband's car. The husband called the police and told the dispatcher that his wife was violent and he was afraid for his safety.

"He opened my car door after dinner, like a gentleman," the woman explained to me, "and said, 'I never should have married you' under his breath. I refused to get into the minivan, and before I turned away from the car, I smacked the rear windshield with my satchel, then walked home a good mile in my new shoes. After all I've been through with him I just wanted to go home where it was calm. And it was peaceful, almost joyful. Then you guys showed up."

The husband insisted he wanted her out, but I knew something was not right. My partner dealt with the husband, and the woman told me resignedly that she was done with all of his violent behavior—she just wanted to get a change of clothes. Her children were inside and she wanted to tell them she'd be ok.

"Do you want to go in?" I asked her. "Or do you want to leave?"

Before she could answer I looked at my partner and the husband and said quickly "this is stupid—Mr. Ryan, do you have a place to go tonight? I think it's best that *you* leave." I knew by the look of relief on the woman's face my instinct was right.

"To Thine Own Self Be True" ~ Shakespeare

I continued to climb the law enforcement leadership ladder, was blessed with an amazing twenty-five year career, and retired as Chief in 2010. It wasn't until I left police work and found my new passion that things began to change—I like to say that coaching found me! My initial intention when I started coaching training was to keep an open mind. What I hadn't counted on—had no freaking idea!—was that my determination, commitment, and willingness to make things happen would create a synergy that changed my life.

We all have a *real* personality that's sometimes overshadowed by who everyone else tells us we should be. I was at a place where the old me didn't fit anymore. It was time to reinvent myself. I didn't want to be numb anymore. It had worked for me in the past, but now I was no longer fulfilled because I was no longer the person I'd started out as. Coaching allowed me to dig deep, peel away those layers, and gave me a whole new life.

I began to let go of the "have to's" and beliefs that no longer served me. I started to hear a small voice in my head (not the "I'm crazy" one!) tell me I wasn't in alignment with who I really am. I paid attention to that voice and made a commitment to embark on a journey to be my *real* self. I thought I was supposed to be this big, strong, powerful, independent person, so I'd worn masks in my relationships out of fear of letting someone into my heart because that felt like weakness to me. Sure, my family saw glimpses of my sappiness over the years, but a whole lot of other people hadn't.

I'm proud to say I'm not the same person I was before. It's like the old me was an oak tree, strong but inflexible, and now I'm a willow tree—just as strong, but empowered through my new-found flexibility. My life is filled with emotion. Still energetic, I continue to get stuff done in a crazy effective way, but with feelings. I can cry and feel ok about it, whereas in the past I'd get pissed at myself for being weak. Now I view vulnerability as being crazy-ass strong!

Alignment with who I *really* am allows me to be passionate about my new career and to live my truth. I now have the tools, skills, and confidence to change people's lives from the inside, but never knew it'd make such a difference in mine. No longer protecting myself *from* myself now I live a life of unlimited possibilities. My senses heightened—I've always been able to see opportunities, but it's like they're on steroids now—my life, previously in black and white with shades of grey, is in *Technicolor!*

My mind is free and, more importantly, my heart is open. I have an amazing girlfriend, and a terrific coaching business, where I help people take their life from good to great, and assist them to get out of their own way. I've learned that I can help people see that they can change when they trust themselves and get comfortable in their own skin. Jeez, I even cry at freaking airports now! For me it's more about feeling a deeper level of love and intimacy than I ever felt before, and that my old choices came from a place of fear rather than love and consciousness. Now I'm so much stronger coming from a place of love by being vulnerable and trusting love and joy...I'm able to be real...

Teaching for iPEC Coaching recently, I told a student from Madison, N.J., that I'd been on the force in neighboring Chatham.

"I know," she said, "you rescued me from my abusive ex-husband seventeen years ago!" At the end of the weekend she told me "when you came that night, you saw through my husband's story. You were the most beautiful thing I ever saw. You radiated strength, and were everything I ever wanted to be, have, know, or touch. And now, here you are rescuing me again—only this time from myself! Thank you!"

I guess I can still be a protector for other people! We come to teach what we need to learn....man, I love this stuff!

ABOUT THE AUTHOR: As Co-Founder of Candy Store Coaching, Karen Sullivan is your no-nonsense partner to help you create the life you want, discover what brings you passion, and fire you up so you can hardly wait for your feet to hit the floor each day. Since Karen's retirement as Chief of Police in 2010, she's been pursuing her passion for helping others understand how their thoughts, feelings and actions can propel them forward, both personally and professionally. Karen is a Certified Professional Coach, an Energy Leadership Index Master Practitioner and instructor for the Institute for Professional Excellence in Coaching (iPEC).

Karen Sullivan
Candy Store Coaching
www.candystorecoaching.com
Karen@candystorecoaching.com
908-868-9892

PART FOUR

Peace, Health
& Well-Being

*"It's also helpful to realize that this very body that we
have, that's sitting right here, right now... with its aches
and its pleasures... is exactly what we need to be
fully human, fully awake, fully alive."*
~ Pema Chedron

The Tear Down Rebuild

Christine Suva

I sat on the bed in the hotel room, tears streaming down my face, exhausted, depressed, and defeated, repeating "I can't do this anymore!" over and over again. During that long night, alone in my hotel room, I barely slept. In and out of wakefulness, I had two incredibly vivid visions. Each lasted only seconds, but they were so powerful and so telling I was literally rocked to my very core.

In the first vision I boarded an airplane and stood near the cockpit next to the pilot. My husband Tom waited on the tarmac outside the door of the plane surrounded by enormous bags of luggage, looking desperate. It was clear he couldn't figure out how to get all of his bags onto the plane to accompany me.

"I'm sorry sir, we'd love to have you onboard, but we can't accommodate all of your bags on this trip," the pilot said calmly. "You have too much weight there."

Immobilized, my feet seemingly cemented to the plane's floor, tears streamed down my face as I pleaded with Tom.

"Please, drop the bags and come with me!" I implored him. "I want you with me, and there's no place for them! You don't need them where we're going! Please...drop the bags!"

"Don't leave me!" begged Tom as tears slid down his cheeks. But he couldn't let go of the bags and step onto the plane.

In the second vision, I neared the top side of a mountain energized, alive, passionate, and tired from the work of the climb— but determined to keep moving upward. I stopped and looked down to the landing where Tom lay on top of bags of gear. Too heavy for him to carry anymore, he was flat on his back with the bags beneath and around him. His hand outstretched toward me, he cried "please don't leave me!" as tears rolled down his face.

I clung to the side of the mountain, exhausted, determined, frozen, and unable to bring myself to go back down though my heart ached. Through the tears, I begged him "please, just leave the bags and come with me! You don't need them up here and I don't have the strength to carry you and them anymore. Please, just come with me—I want you with me!"

The Oxygen Mask

Tom and I met when I was twenty-nine and he was thirty-two. It wasn't only that he was physically attractive and athletic, or that we shared similar interests and that he possessed the drive to create financial success. I fell in love with his heart, integrity, and his rock solid family values. An extremely hard working, humble guy with a strong head for business and a deep desire to be successful, his values matched my own.

"He's a great guy from a wonderful family, but I have to warn you—he hates his job," a mutual friend told me. *No big deal,* I thought, *so he'll change it! After all, that's what I'd do*...already years into a career I loved and happy with myself (imperfections and all), I was ready to set the world on fire!

After we married, I realized that—far from lazy—Tom spent a lot of time listening to his inner bully who beat him up for not being perfect. Coming from the family belief that humbleness is a prized quality, it was difficult for him to acknowledge his true strengths. His poorly handled dyslexia made his early school years difficult, which damaged his self-confidence. Despite this, however, he became a skilled investor and manifested wealth as a young man. But fear of exposure of his dyslexia perpetuated his victim mindset, paralyzed him, and filled him with deep despair. Unaware still of his true life purpose, his current job's poor fit spilled over like poison into our relationship.

Tom placed family before everything else. My rock during four miscarriages, he kept alive hope that we'd be able to have a child when I had difficulty believing it myself. He welcomed my sister and her children into our home during a painful divorce without complaint, and worked long hours to support us at a job that left him exhausted, defeated, and depressed.

Tom's industry was one of the hardest hit at the start of the economic downturn. He went from one of his company's top employees to feeling like the barrel of a gun was pointed directly at his head and he could do no right. Nervous and embarrassed to tell me he feared losing his job—I was a stay-at-home mom with our two young children by then—I told him I supported him come what may. Shortly after, he lost his job.

At the same time, I experienced an overwhelming flow of energy around my own sense of purpose—a deep calling—and decided to reinvent myself as a certified life and career coach. The daughter of a United Methodist Minister and a teacher, caring for others is in my blood. I learned early on how to use my strengths and talents to help others and realized my purpose at a young age. However, along the way I'd absorbed the notion that "business" was only about making money—but I believed it should be more about helping people. This made it difficult for me to charge what I was truly worth.

Tom and other mentors helped open my eyes to this limiting belief. They allowed me to realize that charging what I was worth would not change *who I am,* but rather allow me to be *more of who I am* and serve a wider clientele. Divinely guided toward my future, I threw myself passionately into a year-long training program while Tom took over primary care of our household and children.

As winter set in, so did self-doubt, frustration, and anger at his situation. Tom simultaneously withdrew and clung to his family. I sensed this and desperately attempted to keep him from falling deeper. While the weight of his situation, responsibility for our children, and financial strain bore down heavily, I lived a dichotomy: Absolute passion for my own purpose, and fear and worry for Tom, who was slipping into a deep, dark depression.

All I Need Is The Air That I Breathe...

Three weeks after my visions in that hotel, the crisis hit. My passion for my new field and desire to jump in wholeheartedly prevented me from getting the rest I so desperately needed. Within two weeks, I gutted and painted my office, secured my domain name, filed papers to incorporate my business, and purchased office equipment and furniture. Then our Labrador Retriever died suddenly the following week, adding the burden of grief.

Diagnosed with allergy-induced asthma three years before, I'd never had an actual asthma attack. When my normal medications proved useless, I found myself on round-the-clock steroids and nebulizer breathing treatments. I slept sitting up just to breathe. Meanwhile, I dove into online training for my new business and sat at my laptop with headphones, a breathing mask, and my nebulizer machine for two months until I wound up in the emergency room on intravenous steroids and oxygen.

I needed nine days in the hospital to bring it under control. Told not to talk because I also suffered from frequent laryngitis, it was *forced* rest. I'd pushed for so long, carried so much stress and worry for Tom, and driven myself headlong and so passionately into my new business that I literally crashed and burned! Ironically, my self-censure about the true toll Tom's struggle had taken on me manifested in my inability to speak!

Always deeply connected to my body, I'd completely disconnected from its signals and kept pushing. I did this despite knowing exactly what it felt like to breathe through a cocktail straw and to experience the sheer exhaustion of simply trying to breathe! My perseverance and drive to get past this time in our lives and on to a better future circumvented the reality that my body needed rest and nurturing.

Even though I'd taught stress management and relaxation therapy and studied the mind/body connection, I failed to heed the warnings until my body ended up screaming "enough!" and I found myself lying in that hospital bed.

Lesson Learned

That was my final wakeup call. I had to surrender and turn Tom over to God, pray for his health and peace of mind—and the willingness to do the work to change the thoughts and beliefs that kept him stuck. I realized that, although I maintained healthy boundaries with clients, I took on too much responsibility in my own relationship with Tom.

Intellectually I knew it wasn't wise to absorb so much of his pain and to try to repair what wasn't mine to fix, but emotionally I was driven to help him! My very best friend, I adore Tom and it pained me to see him in such despair. I was determined to push him out of his own way so we could move on! I understood clearly that nothing would change until he surrendered and took responsibility for his own thoughts and beliefs. No amount of pushing or cajoling would change that.

My impatience and desire to help prevented me from taking my own advice, which threw me into a tailspin. It was literally killing me that he stayed stuck for so long! I'd lost my sense of healthy boundaries which resulted in my body breaking down under the stress.

Tom finally reached the point where he knew he had to change...to do the hard work on *himself*, and let go of his limiting beliefs. He began to shift how he viewed himself and the world around him. The difference was amazing as he genuinely embraced the process of raising his level of consciousness, energy, and the law of attraction that I'd tried to teach him for years! My prayers were finally answered!

Tom grew healthier and more empowered, and began to take risks and create a new life, which in turn saved him and our marriage. Our finances had taken a huge hit, but the tradeoff for his health was worth it! Now he's rebuilding his life from the inside out and I'm proud and grateful, as our marriage is stronger and healthier than ever.

I learned the hard way that what doesn't kill me makes me stronger. Lying in that hospital bed, I knew I couldn't give up on myself—I had too much left to give! I see now I needed to respect my own boundaries—especially with those I love—and remember to always put on my own oxygen mask first! Doing so allows me to bring to my coaching *all* of my love, compassion, training, and experience to help others lead happier, healthier, and more fulfilling lives. I know now with conviction that sometimes a tear down is necessary in order to rebuild something far stronger...

ABOUT THE AUTHOR: Christine Suva, a Certified Life and Career Coach (CPC), Energy Leadership Master Practitioner, and Founder of THRIVE Coach Services, Inc., is deeply committed to helping others find passion, purpose and success in their lives! She has over 15 years experience guiding thousands across the country to achieve career and personal goals as an Outplacement Consultant and Wellness Professional. Expert certified in state-of-the-art assessment tools; Christine provides customizable group/one-on-one coaching, motivational speaking, training and consulting. She has a talent for getting to the core of who a person is, what they want, what holds them back, and provides tools and strategies for success!

Christine Suva, President
THRIVE Coach Services, Inc.
www.thrivecoachservices.com
christine@thrivecoachservices.com
630-427-7432

Finding the Light Within

Ericka Crawford

Clean crisp morning air filled my lungs. I breathed rhythmically in and out as oxygen pumped to my legs, and my heart beat in sync with my feet as I pedaled my bike up a long hill near my house. Training for my first hundred-mile bike ride two weeks away, I felt strong and grateful.

Suddenly, a sharp pain in my left knee snapped me out of my rhythm and, when I cranked the pedals again, another sharp pain took my breath away. I clipped out of my pedals quickly and stepped onto the pavement. A rush of fear overwhelmed me.

This can't be happening! I thought. *Not again! Please God, not again! Haven't I suffered enough? Please don't take this away from me!* My mind flashed back to when I'd experienced this same feeling twelve years before.

The summer before my senior year of college, only twelve feet off from qualifying for the Olympic trials in discus throwing, I was determined to train all summer and qualify my senior year. While on my ten-mile morning run—part of my strict training regimen—I was stopped dead in my tracks on mile three as a sharp pain flashed through my left knee.

I massaged my knee for a while and tried to resume my run. But something kept catching in my knee. *How am I going to fix this so I can keep training?* I wondered as I walked back home.

"Mom, I think I need surgery on my knee again, something's not right," I greeted her as I entered the house. Our eyes met and I remember her expression—compassionate but fearful. I knew she was worried about another surgery and long recovery.

Two days later my orthopedic surgeon confirmed that a piece of my knee's patella had broken off and said I needed surgery to remove it. I recall the look of despair on his face as he entered the recovery room following my surgery. He explained calmly that all the wear and tear from athletics and two previous knee surgeries had taken their toll on my knee. Only twenty, my knee was similar to that of someone over fifty!

His next sentence changed the course of my life instantly: "Ericka, if you want to preserve your knee enough to be able to walk by the time you're fifty, you'll have to stop throwing the discus and never run again..."

I was at a loss for words—my Olympic dream was over! Worse yet, I could no longer run...overcome with fear and sadness, anger rushed over me suddenly as tears streamed down my face.

"I know you're on an athletic scholarship," the doctor continued, "and I'll support you as you finish your senior year of college, but you'll have to change your training regimen to swimming and a stationary bike—no more running or stair climbing."

Shattered Dreams

I stood over my bike now and the feeling was eerily similar to the one I'd had lying in that hospital bed twelve years ago. Severe physical pain and emotional anguish filled my days for the next six weeks. I went from riding my bike one hundred and twenty miles a week to walking with a cane. In severe pain, I awaited my surgery. I was told I wouldn't be able to ride my bike more than fifteen to twenty miles three times a week, or walk on uneven surfaces, including the beach and cobblestone. Nor could I hike or perform tasks on my knees such as gardening, cleaning, etc.

The surgery entailed cutting my tibia in half and re-angling my leg fifteen degrees to take the weight off the inside of my knee. Too young for a knee replacement, the goal of the surgery was to buy me ten years until new technology was available. Although this surgery would allow me to walk again, I was skeptical about the doctor's predictions, since I'd been through three previous knee surgeries already and worked my way back to a fulfilling physical life.

It turned out this recovery was far more difficult than I'd anticipated—physically, mentally, and emotionally. I went from the best physical shape ever to a life filled with pain and despair. I lived on ibuprofen for the next seven years to help subdue the severe pain and arthritis in my knee. I'm not sure which was worse—the physical pain or the emotional pain, as my sadness, guilt, and anger at not being able to do all the things my partner and I had dreamed about sank in. I couldn't even walk my dog every day as we'd done together for the past ten years!

I went from being able to walk freely around my workplace and engage with people for any length of time, to standing no more than thirty minutes without severe pain. I remember timing my bathroom breaks. I'd pick something up off the printer and have an ad hoc five minute meeting with co-workers just to limit the time I needed to stand and walk. I remember the despair I felt as I'd take the elevator instead of the stairs to my second floor office. Embarrassed, I wondered what people thought of me for riding the elevator only one floor!

Finally, tired from seven years of pain from my various knee surgeries, stressed from working twelve to fourteen hour days, and having difficulty sleeping, it was clear I'd lost much of my self-confidence and did not feel healthy or happy overall.

The Healing Begins

I was feeling much better about myself that beautiful sunny October day as I entered the Mago Garden Retreat Center in Sedona, where a group of us gathered to reconnect to our inner selves, nature, and each other as citizens of the earth to help create a better world. Although I'd been here before, I hadn't experienced the full extent of positive power of which my subconscious mind and belief system were capable, but that day forever changed my life.

During the previous eight months I'd learned how to open up my meridian channels, and to meditate and heal my knee through "Life Particles," a concept created by meditation expert Ilichi Lee to help describe to others the most elemental particles of the universe. I learned methods of self-healing through Dahn Yoga practices, and went from not being able to walk more than thirty minutes or ride my bike more than fifteen miles at a time, to completing a fifty mile bike ride, climbing Mt. Moak in South Korea, and walking our dog whenever I wanted. My knee still hurt and I'd take ibuprofen when it flared up, but I'd made significant strides in my healing process and felt really great about how much I had grown.

I felt some pain and stiffness in my knee as we began that day and in the middle of a training method called "Brain Wave Vibration"—designed to open up our minds and meridian channels—I connected completely with the rhythm of the music and the energy that flowed through my body. I focused on relieving the pain in my left knee, when a sudden rush of sadness and guilt hit me in the pit of my stomach.

I kept going and intensified my movements to discover the origin of these emotions, when my body became enveloped in anger and rage. A sound from deep in my belly rose to my head and I screamed out in anger. Immediately, as if a cloud had moved aside, I *saw* the origin of my knee pain. Pictures of religious leaders from my childhood appeared before me and shouted: "We are all sinners! You are a sinner if..." They then recited a whole laundry list of sins. "We are not worthy of the kingdom of heaven and the only way to enter is..." their voices continued as the sins they'd listed scrolled through my mind.

Suddenly, calmness drifted over me and an unforgettable clarity emerged. In a flash I realized I'd strived to be the best at everything I did in order to "be good enough and worthy enough!" *How could this be?* I wondered in amazement. *How could I feel I'm not good enough? I have a loving partner, successful career, a good education, friends and family that love me, and material success!*

Then another realization shot through me. I had caused my own physical pain—and the stress in my life—through my continuous need to prove to myself that "I am good enough." At that instant light filled my body, tears streamed down my face, and the pain in my knee released! I saw with sharp clarity how this one belief, buried deep within my subconscious, had shaped my life's journey thus far.

The Morning After

I lay on the floor, exhausted from crying and saying "I'm sorry!" and "Please, forgive me!" over and over again to myself for not believing I was good enough, when a voice inside of me said: *It's going to be okay, I'm here now...I've always been here—you just couldn't hear me. It's time to get up and go create the life you were meant to live—a life of creation, abundance, health, happiness, peace, and joy!*

Deep gratitude filled every cell of my body as I rose from the floor and promised to take action every day to create a life of health, happiness, and peace for myself and others. I realized I never understood how storing emotional pain in my body over the course of my life could take such a toll on me. Now that I'd physically experienced the power of the mind and belief, I learned how to travel inside my body with mind-body training and meditation and release negative energy, emotions, and pain. I realized also that I had created every situation—both good and bad—in my life. Everything that had happened so far in my life was to help get me to this day—a day of awakening my soul to its true nature.

Through my healing process—which included taking full responsibility for my physical condition and creating my own happiness—I significantly increased my confidence and stamina, lost fifty pounds to maintain a healthy body weight, and I continue to awaken my brain every day to a fully conscious life.

Today, I help coach others to discover and actualize their infinite potential so they may return to their natural state of health, happiness, peace, love, abundance, and joy, and lead authentically. My own journey to joy propels me forward with purpose and fills me with light, as I guide others to find their own light within.

ABOUT THE AUTHOR: Transformational leadership and life coach Ericka Crawford teaches individuals how to tap into their infinite potential, and to realize and actualize the life they desire in order to return to their natural state of health, happiness, peace, love, joy, and abundance. Founder of "Light Leadership - Leading from within," Ericka draws from twelve years experience as a coach, mentor, speaker, inspirer, and author, and eighteen years in diagnostics, medical device, pharmaceutical, and biotech companies. She has served three years on the board of directors for the Southern California Healthcare Business Women's Association and is a Dahn Master (Energy Principle Yoga and Meditation Instructor).

Ericka Crawford
Light Leadership
www.light-leadership.com
ericka@light-leadership.com
760-212-4099

The Other Side of the White Coat

Dr. Stephanie Kabongo

Everything's upside down and inside out! Calm and composed on the outside, inside it's as if I've awakened to a bizarre world where everything is completely reversed, and it's freaking me out!

Surrounded in my hospital room by my mother, friends, flowers, and get well cards, I'm scared, even though I know *a lot* about medicine and my impending operation. Here I am, admitted to the hospital with an intravenous needle stuck in my arm! Here I am, *a doctor* in a hospital bed getting a taste of my own medicine—literally! No doctor in the world expects that one day she'll become *the patient* on the consent forms!

Is this my new reality? I wonder nervously. *Since when am I on the other side of the white coat?*

Working as an emergency medicine doctor in busy hospitals had both its perks and its detrimental effects. For me the price came at the expense of my deteriorating hip joint. I naturally had an unsteady hip from a childhood condition, and spent eight months in a full-length leg cast during puberty to treat the condition. I remained with some unsteadiness in that joint and was never cured completely.

Now in my late twenties, my pre-operation hip x-rays showed advanced deterioration of a worn-out joint. My joint had stiffened to the point where walking even short distances became difficult, and my hip looked worse than that of an old lady! Climbing stairs involved holding on to the rails for dear life. My orthopaedic surgeon originally suggested he operate on the whole bone, but I refused. Still young, I was not about to have a part of myself removed.

Contrary to popular belief, being a doctor doesn't automatically mean healthy eating habits—doctors need to make an effort to be healthy just like the rest of the population. I changed my diet in preparation for the operation, and continued to exercise even though it was uncomfortable. I aimed to set my body up to rebuild and heal itself as much as possible before the operation—to do my part and provide my body with the nutrition it needed to accomplish this.

I signed the consent form to have my hip operation performed despite my uneasy feelings. This role reversal—being the patient instead of the doctor—left me unsettled and more than a little bit threatened, as if my world was crumbling before my very eyes...

Now I lay on the bed waiting for the doctors to treat me as a patient while on their ward round, when suddenly I realized to my horror that my "MD" title was omitted from my chart!

I'm just another patient on their clipboard file with a hospital number and a diagnosis as far as they're concerned! I thought. *Patient Stephanie Kabongo, nothing more!* How truly bizarre to be treated like a normal patient instead of a privileged one because of the missing "MD" title next to my name!

During my entire medical career as a fully trained doctor, I was always the one in charge of everything—the treatments, decisions, and patient care. I'd never imagined for a second what it was like to be *the patient!* Now I lay here—on the other side of the doctor-patient relationship—feeling disempowered and hopeless. I was *the patient* with no authority, just me, and I wasn't the one making treatment decisions. Instead, I was the one receiving medical orders and instructions!

A Taste of My Own Medicine

Day two of my hip operation was life changing for me. When the doctors came to my cubicle they had no idea I was a doctor just like them. They spoke amongst themselves, and addressed the file on my clipboard more than me.

They presented my case: "Miss Stephanie, day two, post-hip surgery, wound healing well...she is ready for rehabilitation and physiotherapy, possible discharge in two days,"—all while the wound on my hip was exposed! The whole ward round was done so quickly that, before I could ask any questions, they'd moved on to the next patient.

How dare they not treat me like a person? I fumed. Disgusted and angry, I couldn't believe how horrible it felt to be treated like a file on a clipboard! Suddenly I had an "oh my God!" moment that distracted me from my anger. My eyes opened wide and my jaw dropped. I couldn't speak. I stared at their backs as they walked from patient to patient in our four-bed room.

I realized during that horrible moment that I—a doctor at that very same time in my life—performed my hospital ward rounds and treated my patients *exactly* as these doctors had just treated me! Ward rounds had never been too important to me—they were something I had to get over and done with so I could go to the clinic or the operating room.

I never took the time to think about how I came across to my patients. Just like these doctors, I performed my ward rounds very quickly and didn't leave much time to allow patients to ask me questions early on these mornings. My professional behaviour was just like theirs!

I never once thought about how dismissive it feels to be examined and consulted with so speedily, even though the patient's been looking forward to seeing one of her doctors for hours. The sudden shock of realizing that my own patients felt like crap, just as I did now, was unbearable! I couldn't breathe as I watched these doctors speed through their patient rounds, and a horrible hollow feeling hit my heart. I now know what it means when people say their heart has been broken—I felt that way now!

Even though I always thought I was doing the best I could for my patients physically and medically, it was difficult for me to come to terms with the fact that I might not have been doing much good for them emotionally or mentally.

That morning proved to be a significant milestone in my health career. It changed me, not just as a doctor but as a person. I was present in that moment like no other moment in my life! I knew my life had changed in that instant, and I asked my mother to take a photo of me. I never wanted any patient of mine to experience the lack of emotional support I did that morning!

I made a decision to always honour my patients' emotional, mental, *and* spiritual wellness just as much as their physical treatments. I decided to be a compassionate human being—first and foremost!—before acting as a doctor.

Break

I went into that hospital with such a negative state of mind, but what happened while I was there changed my outlook on life, health, God, and the universe! Every cell in the human body has a lifespan and renews itself every two, five, and ninety days of our lives. Knowing this motivated me to visualise healing happening in my body before the operation.

The operation itself proved a success, as indeed my bones began the healing process just as I'd prayed for and visualised. I kept affirming to myself that "healing is possible and is already happening..." It is one thing to know human physiology and another to actually apply these principles to your life. I increased my intake of calcium, magnesium, and vitamin D prior to my operation, as magnesium helps to relax the muscles. While the patients around me were stressed out, I was much calmer!

Six weeks of physiotherapy and rehabilitation treatments at home proved a blessing, and I used that time to research and study integrative medicine, holistic approaches to medical treatments, nutrition for weight loss, and mind-body medicine. Further studies on health and healing lead me not only to medical books but to people like Dr Deepak Chopra (whom I admire deeply), and Dr John Demartini, an expert on the human mind and physiology. I read Anthony Robbins also, and studied herbal medicine.

Those six weeks gave me the time out I needed and paved the foundation for my 5 Star Health & Wellness online coaching program for weight loss and health, and my book *The 5 Star Health & Wellness Program.* Today I run my new and improved method of patient care, and am thankful for my experience in the hospital as a patient which led me to build my reputation as a successful health coach. My online health programs assist clients to lose weight, increase health and energy, and provide natural treatments for chronic dis-eases. I supplement my online programs with group coaching and one-on-one private clients all over the world.

I thank my creator and my almighty saviour for the experience in the hospital that day that changed my life for the better. Now a wiser and more informed health and wellness coach, I help transform thousands of people's lives. I know also that healing is always possible and that everything always happens for a reason. I have seen both sides of the white coat, and now dedicate my life and work to being mindful of integrating and strengthening the medical and spiritual mind/body connection for the purpose of health and healing...

ABOUT THE AUTHOR: Dr. Stephanie K is a medical doctor and a health and success coach. As a world-leading authority on health & success breakthrough, she is passionate about assisting people to lose weight, achieve success goals and to live a stress-free life through holistic success coaching and natural health .... no matter where they start from. Dr. Stephanie's core mission is to help people eliminate struggle, failures and un-healthiness and to live successful and stress-free lives! With the help of her using simple and effective techniques, Dr. Stephanie's clients overcome their struggles, stress and burn out to regain health, success, happiness and vitality!

Dr. Stephanie Kabongo
drstephaniek@gmail.com
South Africa
+27 72 580 8864

Joy is a Beach
Kathy Fyler

The waves crashed into the thirty-foot seawall and sent salt water high into the air and over the two-lane road separating my parent's house from Long Island Sound. High tide that day looked like the ocean might flow right over the top of the wall and engulf the street and the houses on it. The wind gusted up to 100 mph and the rain pelted down almost horizontally. It was nearly impossible to stand outside and watch, but I did it anyway.

Video shot of me moving out from behind the protection of the house to face the wind head-on made me look like the guy on *The Weather Channel*. It took every ounce of strength I had not to be knocked over or lifted up by its amazing power. Mesmerized and awestruck—despite the imminent danger—it was breathtakingly beautiful.

We survived the night without power and in the morning, incredibly, the sound was as placid and calm as a lake. The sun was shining and the seawall seemed as protective as ever as the water barely reached its bottom. This complete transformation in a mere twenty-four hours proved to be an incredible statement about the wonder of Mother Nature.

The energy of the ocean—both peaceful and chaotic—called to me.

I've always loved the beach—whether I was sunbathing on a hot summer day, taking long walks, or watching the waves during a big storm. Vacations that included skiing or mountains were not my thing. I chose always to travel to places that included sand, surf, and a beach. Some of my favorite vacations were to Puerto Rico, where beautiful velvet sandy beaches meet gorgeous aqua blue water that's crystal clear and warm. There I felt at peace and grounded—full of joy!

I imagined that one day down the road I'd find a home near the ocean and be able to experience this bliss on a daily basis. But early in my life I'd somehow absorbed the idea that I could only live at the beach (a.k.a., the "seashore" in Connecticut where I grew up) if I was very wealthy or retired. This limiting belief held me back from ever believing I could live at the shore at this time in my life—not retired and definitely not rich!

Movin' On

My partner and I planned to move in 2009. The warm weather of the south appealed to us, and we thought about moving to North Carolina or Florida. At that time we lived in northern New Jersey and my family in Connecticut was close by. Unsure where I wanted to go, moving and living that far away seemed unsettling and I didn't feel it was the right time to move south. We ran our business from home, so we could live anywhere (except by the beach because that was reserved only for retired and/or wealthy people!) So we continued to search neighboring towns to find the perfect place.

One day I looked on Craigslist and located a house for rent in Cape May, N.J. I was only exploring, and although this house was a few hours from where we currently lived, it looked amazing. The rent was reasonable, too, so much so that I thought it was a misprint, or perhaps that the rent listed was weekly, not monthly. I figured I had nothing to lose, so I responded.

A few days later, the owner answered: The rent was per month and it was available! *Should we go look at it?* I wondered. *Is it too far away?* Then my monkey mind chimed in: *Cape May is a beach town!* I still held that nagging belief that only the rich lived close to the water. However, it was perfect, and when all of the pieces fell into place the decision was easy.

The Jersey Shore

Moving to the beach became a reality that February. Not only was this house near the water, it contained many of my "wish list" items: granite countertops; an open floor plan; lots of windows; a fireplace in the living room *and* the bedroom; a large soaking tub; a huge walk-in shower with two shower heads; and even a dumbwaiter we named Lola! *How exciting!* But best of all was the view of the Delaware Bay! I could sit in the living room, dining room, family room, or kitchen and be reminded of the amazing ocean!

Local access to the beach was right across the street! I remember the first day we walked down this path to the sandy shore. Cold and wintery that day, my eyes became teary in the blustery wind and I could barely catch my breath—I can still feel how wonderful it was to be that close to the water and behold the energy of the sea.

We actually lived just outside of Cape May—close enough to enjoy its quaintness but far enough away to miss the traffic and crowds the summer season attracted. Family and friends visited to experience with us this wonderful home and location. I felt lucky and blessed.

As we enjoyed "beach life" I thought, *if we could manifest this, we can manifest anything. If living across the street from the water feels like this, how great would it be to live directly on the beach?* But my old belief that only the rich can have beach homes reared its ugly head. *No, it's too expensive,* I told myself. *If we found a place we could afford, it would probably be too small...*

Because I'd manifested with such ease this recent move, I began to learn to release beliefs that did not serve me. So I set the following intention: I'd like to live in an oceanfront home with no obstructed views that I can easily afford.

And in the fall of 2011, that's exactly what I received—an opportunity to live in a four-bedroom house on the Atlantic Ocean with beautiful floor-to-ceiling, wall-to-wall windows—*literally* right on the beach! The owner, who wanted income for the entire winter season, made us an "offer we couldn't refuse."

The house in Sea Isle City, N.J., was ours to live in until April 2012. So magnificent and colorful were the sunrises there that I looked forward to waking up at six a.m. just to see them. At night, the moon's reflection glistened on the water and seemed to flow in pathways directly to me. During the day the sun sparkled on the waves that rolled continuously onto the shore.

It was time to decide—and manifest—our next move. The year before, we'd been on a business trip to Indian Shores, Florida, just outside Tampa on the Gulf of Mexico. A magical place, we took long walks on the beach, watched incredible sunsets, and enjoyed the local fresh seafood and laid-back ambiance. There was something about the energy of southwest Florida that kept calling to me.

Even though I had reservations about moving far from family in Connecticut, I was tired of northeast winters. I didn't enjoy shoveling snow or the frigid cold. And the summers always seemed too short. I reminded myself I could work from anywhere—I was ready to make the move...

The Sunshine State

When we decided to see if we liked Florida as a more permanent location, we found an "off season" condo easily and set our sights on living there temporarily. This meant we could stay through December— plenty of time to "test the waters." We packed our possessions into a U-Haul trailer and headed south to Marco Island.

On our second travel day, we stopped in Georgia to eat. Back on the road we discovered the car wasn't running quite right. It started to slow down and wouldn't go faster than twenty mph. *Oh no*, I thought, *is this a sign? Maybe we're not meant to move so far away!*

We called AAA and had the car towed to the next exit. Afraid that pulling the trailer all the way from New Jersey might have been too much for my ten year-old SUV, luckily we'd simply run out of oil. The car's protective mechanism shuts down the engine to prevent any damage when it runs out of oil. Five quarts of oil for the car and a chocolate milkshake for Sue, and we were good to go. Back on the road.

We crossed the Marco Island Bridge the next day into our new "paradise." My fears erased themselves quickly as I took in the beauty and tranquility of this tropical setting, and we settled into the cutest condo across the street from the Gulf of Mexico. Imagine that...I'd released my limiting belief and, within a few years, I lived on the Delaware Bay, the Atlantic Ocean—and now the Gulf of Mexico! Quite a journey...

Epilogue

After a wonderful year in southwest Florida, we've decided this is where we want to be—for now. Its beauty has surpassed all of my expectations and it was a nice surprise to learn that my family wanted to follow me to Florida. They now live only minutes away!

This journey to beautiful southwest Florida has taught me several lessons: I must continue to follow my heart, release those voices in my head that do not serve me, and I cannot let fear stop me in my tracks. I've learned that doing what I love brings me joy, and that joy is a beach!

ABOUT THE AUTHOR: Kathy Fyler's earlier diverse career includes being a Critical Care Nurse, Project Manager for a technology firm, and owner of a $5 million manufacturing company. In 2005, Kathy felt a calling to make "more of a contribution to what matters most in this world". Using her experience and passion for technology and people, she co-founded Powerful You! Women's Network and Powerful You! Publishing to fulfill her personal mission of assisting women in creating connections via the internet, live meetings and the published word. Kathy loves to travel the country connecting with the inspiring women of Powerful You!

Kathy Fyler
Powerful You! Inc.
www.powerfulyou.com
kathy.fyler@powerfulyou.com

The Bare Minimum
Victoria Pilotti

What a high! How thrilling to walk down the runway and hear the applause as the mistress of ceremonies describes my outfit—not at all how I felt moments before in the changing room where I'd tried to hide my mastectomy bra and prostheses when I undressed. Never in my wildest imagination did I think that volunteering as a model in a fashion show fundraiser for my son's high school could turn out to be such a healing experience.

Diagnosed with breast cancer months earlier, at first I was in denial.

There's no visible tumor, so I can't have cancer, I rationalized, even though the radiologist pointed to micro-calcifications on the film that had changed from last year's mammography. Breast micro-calcifications—calcium deposits within breast tissue—are common on mammograms and are usually non-cancerous or benign. But certain patterns of calcification—such as tight clusters with irregular shapes—may indicate breast cancer. And my doctor didn't like the changes she saw on my mammogram.

When I showed my husband Eric the radiology report that said "suspicious for malignancy," he marveled at my state of calm. Calm? I was *definitely* in denial. There was no visible mass (tumor) on the mammography, so I *couldn't* have cancer. Then I read a medical study that noted that only thirty-six percent of changes in micro-calcifications were cancerous. My denial was confirmed. *I must be one of the sixty-four percent that do not have cancer,* I reasoned.

Within a few days, reality set in and I scheduled an appointment to see a breast surgeon for a biopsy. I would take the half-hour wait for mammography results any day over the agonizing wait for the biopsy surgeon's phone call, which came three days later at ten p.m.—I didn't think doctors called so late...

"I'm so very sorry," said the voice on the other end of the line.

"It's cancer. Call my office to schedule an appointment."

Double Or Nothing

"If you were my wife, I'd want you to have a lumpectomy," the biopsy surgeon argued when I insisted on a mastectomy. But he could only give me a seventy-five percent guarantee that a lumpectomy would remove all the cancer.

I'd sooner commit suicide than endure the ordeal of a second surgery, I thought, as I sat on my bed night after night reading the pathology report. It said "no clear margins"—meaning there were cancer cells all around the biopsied breast tissue.

While the biopsy surgeon strongly recommended a lumpectomy but couldn't guarantee that I would not need a second surgery for a mastectomy, I knew I needed a second opinion. The second surgeon strongly recommended a mastectomy. With two opposite surgery options, I sought the opinion of a third breast surgeon at Memorial Sloan-Kettering Cancer Center, who also recommended a mastectomy. I scheduled my surgery with him.

However, before long I had second thoughts. I hadn't felt comfortable at Sloan-Kettering and really liked the second surgeon, Dr. Mills, with whom I felt a greater rapport.

"What!?" screamed Eric. "You cancelled your surgery? Stop listening to other people! You were all set at a world-renowned cancer hospital—why did you have to listen to my sister that Dr. Mills accepts our insurance and the other doctor does not? Who cares about the money? So what if your friends think Dr. Mills is a great surgeon!"

"I didn't feel a connection with the surgeon at Sloan-Kettering," I argued. "And it's not the hospital that's important—it's the surgeon! Dr. Mills answered all my questions before I even asked them!"

Eric calmed down and spoke softly, his voice cracking: "I just want you to live...please don't die on me..."

Next I took my surgery decision a step further and requested a bilateral mastectomy to have both breasts removed. It was important to me to be done with breast cancer and mammograms and never again have to wonder whether or not the other breast had cancer. Now I had to convince Dr. Mills that I wanted both breasts removed.

"Are you absolutely certain?" he asked, and then told me he couldn't remove a healthy breast without just cause.

"Can you guarantee I won't be diagnosed with cancer in the other breast?" I asked. Of course, he could not. "There's no way I can go through the agony of waiting for the radiologist to examine another mammography, or live in fear of a doctor calling with negative biopsy results," I explained. "I've never been so sure of anything in my life! If I need cancer surgery for the other breast five, ten, or fifteen years from now, I'll go insane!"

He heard enough. We scheduled the bilateral mastectomy surgery. It was time to tell my children and my parents.

The Aftermath

While still in the hospital post-surgery, Dr. Mills made a follow up visit.

"I know you feel on top of the world," he began. "But you know you need to see an oncologist."

"I have no breasts—why do I need to see an oncologist?" I asked, adamant that I needed no further treatment. "There is no cancer."

A week later in Dr. Mills' office to discuss the mastectomy pathology report, I was told that "less than one millimeter from the fascia" was of great concern. This meant that cancer cells were found less than a thin pencil line away from the muscle tissue.

"Local recurrence—the spread of cancer cells into nearby areas—is ugly," said Dr. Mills. He urged me to schedule a consultation with an oncologist. And so began the next phase of cancer treatment decisions.

During my recuperation from surgery, and before I returned to my job as a high school English as a Second Language (ESL) teacher, Eric suggested I join the high school Mother's Club. I sat at my first meeting wearing a shirt with two pocket flaps to hide where my breasts used to be. I hadn't been fitted yet for a mastectomy bra and prostheses. Too soon, my skin was still sensitive and needed time to heal. I chose not to have breast reconstruction—the plastic surgery options were more frightening to me than the cancer surgery itself! By the third meeting I was nominated to the executive board to help plan fundraising events.

Shortly after that, Eric urged me to attend a function focused on education in New York City of The Italians of American Heritage, a non-profit organization that met in our own neighborhood. I attended several events, and was invited to join their executive board. Thus began my path of volunteering.

My surgery behind me now, future treatment choices proved overwhelming. Although there were no studies with mastectomy patients about the effectiveness of radiation treatment, I decided to have radiation therapy—often recommended for lumpectomy surgeries. I cried every day on the radiation table. *Can the radiation accidentally destroy my heart?* I wondered. *Is it damaging my lungs? Why am I doing this?"*

"If you had chemotherapy, you'd probably be in menopause and your estrogen levels would be lower," the oncologist told me. At each visit he chided me for not accepting chemotherapy as a treatment. My breast cancer was estrogen positive which can progress more rapidly in pre-menopausal women and, conversely, more slowly in post-menopausal women.

I agreed to take Tamoxifen to block the estrogen, in addition to injections to put me into menopause. Immediately these triggered night sweats, hot flashes, sleep deprivation, and mood changes. Gradually, I learned to cope with these disruptions and once again take charge of my life.

Knowledge is Power

Eric also encouraged me to join the National Organization of Italian American Women, where I mentored a college student and helped her to make career decisions. At this organization's annual women's awards dinner, I met Ann Jawin, founder of the Center for the Women of New York. The center's goals are to empower women through equal employment rights and protection from domestic violence. Ann convinced me to join the board and focus my energies on helping to empower high school girls.

I began to discover through volunteering and fundraising that my ideas were warmly accepted and validated, and how wonderful it felt to give and to work together with other caring women who shared a common goal. Many of them became part of my new circle of friends and acquaintances.

Eventually, through the Center for the Women of New York I was introduced to Zonta International, a non-governmental organization (NGO) affiliated with the United Nations. Zonta's mission is to advance the status of women and girls worldwide. When a Zonta member recruited me as a volunteer facilitator for Child Abuse Prevention Services of Long Island, I was happy to help. I presented child abuse and bullying prevention workshops in first grade through eighth grade classrooms in Nassau County public schools, by far my most rewarding volunteer experience to date.

I realize now that I owe so much to my encounter with mortality. Without it, I'd still be doing the same old things, day in and day out. Now I am enthusiastic about the future. I think: *Ok, I had this near death experience, but I'm full of life now! I'm not just going to come home, cook dinner, and go back to my job tomorrow. There's more I have to give—I want to use my time to give back, to do something to help people...*

Forced to make difficult and unconventional treatment decisions, I have no regrets! Ironically, through my breast cancer diagnosis and treatment I've enriched my life by volunteering at women's organizations, Italian cultural associations, and educational conferences—a most positive and fulfilling use of my energy. How wonderful to make a contribution to the greater good!

I look back now on my volunteer contributions with great pride. I helped initiate the first scholarships awarded to high school students either of Italian-American descent or studying the Italian language who demonstrate outstanding community service. Post-cancer, I realized how strongly I felt about the negative stereotype that all Italians must be connected with organized crime, and now work hard to help replace this image by emphasizing the many cultural contributions made by Italian-Americans.

"And our next model is wearing..." Twelve years later I'm back on the runway and in such a different place in my life! In addition to my many volunteer involvements, I've earned a doctorate in education, and my latest venture—attending Toastmasters International local meetings—is helping to improve my communication skills to make my efforts to advocate for women and education even more effective.

I tell everyone at this year's fashion show how the wonderful women of the Mother's Club became such an integral part of my breast cancer healing, and how—without the words "suspicious for malignancy" on my mammography report in August 2000—I might still be going through life doing only the bare minimum...

ABOUT THE AUTHOR: Victoria Pilotti, Ed.D., a New York City public high school English-as-a-second language teacher, has taught graduate courses at St. John's University and Hunter College, and facilitated numerous workshops for teachers at international, national, state, and city conferences. Victoria advises and advocates for women diagnosed with breast cancer, and her husband Eric counsels spouses and sons. A member and officer of the Toast of Queens public speaking club of Toastmasters International since 2007, she has presented over thirty formal speeches (www.toastmasters.org.) Victoria is an active member of www.zonta.org empowering women and girls internationally, and in the N.Y.C. area www.cwny.org enhancing women's rights and health.

Victoria Pilotti
VPilotti.CWNY@gmail.com

Sixty-Five Pounds of Pure Love!

Jodie Penn

Twelve hours all to myself—just me and my iMac! How great is that! No distractions. No boss to yell at me for no reason, no annoying co-workers to bug me. No one to stop by my office to chat, no friends to keep me smiling—*Wait! What?* No friends?

I left my full-time job, excited to grow my freelance work into a full-fledged business. Clients came out of nowhere and soon I had plenty of work to keep me busy. The only thing I hated about working from home was the loneliness. My husband John left for work at eight-thirty a.m. and most nights didn't return until eight-thirty p.m. I couldn't wait for him to get back, and felt sad when he left again each morning. I realized also how much I missed my friends at work! They were the ones who helped each day fly by, and who made getting up and going to work every day worthwhile.

John and I decided to live in an apartment halfway between each of our employers when we first got married. Now that I worked from home, most of my friends and family lived an hour away. I didn't find the people in our complex very friendly—I'd smile and say hello, but all I'd get in return were grunts and glares. Plus most of them worked in the city, which made our complex a ghost town during the day.

I'd grown up in a neighborhood where people were friendly and would do pretty much anything for anyone, so I wasn't used to this! Hold up Dorothy—we're not in Kansas anymore! Kind of a shock to my system! So, for twelve hours a day, I was alone...*really alone.* Not quite what I had in mind...within a few months I teetered on the verge of depression. Something needed to change...finally one day I called John at work and proposed a solution.

"I'm lonely; can we get a dog?" I asked.

"Wow, that's a great idea!" he replied. Yay, he was on board!

We both grew up with dogs, but neither of us had owned one as an adult. I'd always wanted an English bulldog—I loved their squishy faces and laidback attitudes! It must have been meant to be, because John had recently fallen in love with a client's bulldog—he thought she was pretty awesome and so became enthusiastic about looking for one to adopt.

Too Good To Be True

Since our apartment complex only allowed dogs eighteen months or older, I started hunting online for an adult bulldog who needed a home. I found a non-profit called HeavenSent Bulldog Rescue through petfinder.com. HeavenSent is an all-volunteer group of bulldog lovers whose mission is to find homes for bulldogs who are surrendered by their owners, or find themselves otherwise without homes. Many land in animal shelters or wander the streets as strays. The rescue relies solely on donations and fundraisers to finance the veterinary care of bulldogs in need.

Up for adoption through HeavenSent was the cutest dog named Rocco. I filled out the application, said a little prayer, and hit the submit button. When we didn't hear anything, I went back on petfinder.com to look around. Each time I'd look, a female named Margie came up in my searches and I'd read her listing every time. There was something about her little face...soon I fell in love with a dog I'd never met!

She was up for adoption through an all-breed rescue and I was tempted to apply with them, but didn't want to get too many applications out there. A few weeks later I received an email from HeavenSent inviting us to a meet-and-greet at a pet store about forty-five minutes south of us. I was so nervous that Saturday morning—what if they didn't like us? This was our chance to make an impression and show we had the time and the love to devote to a bulldog in need!

It was very busy in the pet store, lots of people visiting the rescue table, getting info, meeting the volunteers, and petting the available dogs. I was in my glory! I'd never been around that many bulldogs before and they were all so different! John and I sat on the floor and Lola, an English bulldog, climbed in my lap and kissed my face!

It was *awesome!* She ran happily between the two of us, kissing our faces and accepting our hugs.

The wonderful volunteers at HeavenSent make it a point to learn what each bulldog needs in his or her perfect forever home, and they told us they felt Lola needed a yard and lots of room in which to run and play. Our apartment was not going to cut it for her. Sad, John and I understood, but I'll never forget her and how she filled me with joy when she jumped into my lap! *This is exactly what I need!* I thought.

Next we met Gizmo. Much mellower, Gizmo was a better fit for our lifestyle. We left the meet-and-greet thinking we were going to foster-to-adopt Gizmo, but unfortunately it wasn't meant to be. One of the volunteers called two days later to tell us that, after getting to know Gizmo better, they felt she needed a yard. Darn, we weren't a match! However, the volunteer told us there was another bulldog in a shelter in northern New Jersey that needed a home.

When we received an email with this bulldog's write-up and pictures, I couldn't believe my eyes—it was Margie, the same dog I'd been following online for a couple of weeks! Two days later Margie visited us with one of the HeavenSent Bulldog Rescue volunteers to inspect our home. John and I met them downstairs, and as soon as Margie's nubby tail started wagging, it was love at first sight! Tears ran down my cheeks—I knew she was ours!

My Little Margie

Basically, Margie was a mess. Twenty pounds underweight, she suffered from ear and eye infections and a strange sore on her elbow. A stray found roaming the streets of Manhattan, Margie was captured and taken to a shelter. From there she landed in an all breed rescue run out of a house. One of twenty-five dogs in crates waiting for a home, she was miserable there. HeavenSent to the rescue!

Our home passed inspection and immediately Margie found the bed we bought for her. She plopped down in it, comfortable as can be, and it was clear she wasn't going anywhere! We were her *fur*-ever family and she was home!

That first night we tried at least thirty different names—Margie didn't fit our precious girl! Plus, she didn't respond to that name. Nothing seemed to be perfect for her, so we stuck with Margie for the time being. Still without a new name, I brought her up to meet my family and their dog Shasta two days later. It was important that the dogs got along and liked each other because my mom and I worked together now.

Margie had been living on the streets for so long, eating whatever she could find, that her digestive system was out of whack. She had the most horrible gas and could clear a room with one toot! Upon meeting my dad, she let one fly.

"She just floated an air biscuit!" he exclaimed.

"*Biscuit!*" I yelled, elated. "That's it! Her name is Biscuit!" And it stuck! After a week on decent food, Biscuit's gas disappeared and soon her smell matched her sweet personality...

Each month we found ourselves hopping in the car to ride down to the HeavenSent meet-and-greet. The volunteers welcomed us and loved watching Biscuit adjust into her new life and become a *real* part of our family. It took a while but, with some TLC and proper treatment, all of Biscuit's health issues cleared up. She gained some much-needed weight and quickly went from forty-four pounds to a healthy sixty-five pounds!

Biscuit loved her new life as a couch potato, and adopted the leather chair in our living room as her own. That chair is now known as Biscuit's chair and you better not sit in it—even if she's all comfy on the couch! She'll get off the couch, stand in front of you, and stomp her feet until you get out of her chair! I love our sixty-five pound lump of pure love—she's just what I need to keep me company, crack me up, and make me smile!

Adopted By The Rescuers!

Later that year the volunteers at HeavenSent asked if we'd conduct a home visit for them because they had a potential adoptive family in our area. We were thrilled and incredibly grateful that they picked us to be Biscuit's family, so of course we jumped at the chance to help them

Little did we know that this home visit would be the start of something amazing. Shortly afterward, HeavenSent Bulldog Rescue adopted *us* as volunteers and the experience has been so rewarding! We joined their other volunteers to help provide foster care, to help with fundraising for veterinary care and rehabilitation, and to help find adoptive families. From home visits and fundraising events to transporting and fostering bulldogs in need, I found what my life was missing: The joy of helping these wonderful dogs find their way and, ultimately, their forever homes!

I've met amazing people along the way and made several lasting friendships. My lonely days are gone! Between my wonderful husband, our two precious bulldogs (how could we resist another?), and all the wonderful rescued bulldogs that cross my path, my heart is full of joy! I'll never forget how it all started with the one who still cracks me up and always keeps me smiling—my sixty-five pounds of pure love!

ABOUT THE AUTHOR: Jodie Penn is a multi-faceted woman. Her passions are family, art, helping others and her two bulldogs – Biscuit and Brody. After years of working as a Creative Director in Corporate America, she left to partner with her mom to create AlphaZelle, a company dedicated to bringing the cleanest and healthiest skin care, personal care, baby, household and pet care products to the marketplace. Jodie educates people about toxic ingredients found in everyday products and provides a safe alternative. Jodie is an avid volunteer for HeavenSent Bulldog Rescue and is a partner in Penn Creative Group, a graphic design company, with her husband John.

Jodie Penn
Artist, Graphic Designer, Entrepreneur
www.AlphaZelle.com
Jodie@AlphaZelle.com
973-224-2058

Spiritual Nourishment
Michelle Renee Johnson

I stood sideways in front of the full-length mirror in my cramped college apartment and began to cry silent, painful tears of resignation. At five foot six and one hundred and ten pounds, most would view what they saw in the mirror triumphantly. I felt only pure, utter hopelessness.

Later I'd joke that—as a bulimic—I was simply a failed anorexic. But in this space, in the deepest depth of my eating disorder, humor was a foreign concept. The focus of my despair was my stomach, more than likely distended from digestive upset and malnutrition than fat, but when it came to my body image, I was far from rational.

The Loss of Inner Joy

I don't recall exactly when my love-hate relationship with food began, but I remember secretly devouring an entire box of Girl Scout cookies to comfort myself after my supposed middle school "best friend" convinced everyone in our circle of friends not to talk to me anymore. Episodes similar to this unfolded through high school, including finding solace in an entire tray of homemade rice crispy treats when the boy I liked didn't invite me to the school dance. Every episode was followed by the physical pain of overindulgence and the subsequent hiding of the proof of my guilty pleasure.

The alternative—asking for comfort and support from friends or family for my perceived "petty" issues—never seemed justified. Rather, it always appeared my closest friends and family needed me to be solid, stable, and supportive to help *them* deal with much bigger issues. How could I share my heartbreak over the latest boy who didn't notice me when my mother counseled abused and neglected children, my sister was bullied and depressed, and my closest friends faced their own emotional overload as a result of divorce, incest, abuse, and other significantly more painful issues?

Sugary food became my silent comfort as my self-judgment grew. By mid-high school I learned the art of climbing the social ladder to gain the external validation I thought I needed to fill the expanding emptiness inside. I'd often compromise many of my internal values in the process, which only caused the empty hole to grow even larger.

The stressors of college initiated even more destructive behavior, including late nights of beer, marijuana, and fast food, along with the horrific realization that my "skinny" genes were no longer able to manage the heavy load of caloric intake. Skipping a meal or two seemed the logical solution to help me drop the unexpected "freshman fifteen," but when the need for comfort struck, I'd overindulge yet again.

Late one night during the end of my freshman year, I sat in my bathroom—bloated, sick and disgusted with myself for overeating once again—when I hit upon a logical solution. I'd simply throw up the food to get it out before it caused more damage—just this once, of course...

Over time, the daily binging and purging of bulimia began to take its toll. I started to lose my hair, experience constant heartburn, and strained my diaphragm from all that heaving. Never mind the time and energy it took to avoid eating meals with others, or to find a quiet place to throw up if meals couldn't be avoided! A few months into it I realized this wasn't a great long-term solution, but felt I had no other alternative. I couldn't seem to stop overeating and I definitely wasn't willing to gain weight! Besides, people would think of me as a drama queen; after all, I had no sordid past or horrific life experience to justify my eating disorder.

Remembering True Joy

A little over a year into my addiction, as I stood in front of that mirror and looked at my bloated stomach—feeling lonely, miserable, and exhausted—the final pebbles in my crumbling wall of justification gave way. I finally had to admit that this eating disorder controlled my entire life. I arrived officially at rock bottom...

The silent tears of resignation transformed into deep, uncontrollable sobs. *Can I even call this level of misery living?* I wondered. *Is life even worth living with all this pain?* I cried until no more tears would come. Eventually I arrived at a place of stillness and tearless exhaustion, and a thought arose: *I can't remember the last time I felt happy.* I didn't mean the euphoric reaction to a man complimenting my looks, or the numbing joy of inebriation, but the kind of natural happiness that bubbles up from within. *It's been eons,* I thought sadly.

Suddenly I flashed to a memory of myself at about eight or nine years old, sneaking outside early one summer morning before everyone else awakened. Still in my nightgown, with beautiful childhood innocence, I laid down giddily on the warm concrete of my front walkway just to soak up the sun's warm rays. Feeling the cool morning breeze rustle over my skin, I reveled in the sounds of summer all around me. Eventually, fully warmed and getting hungry, I snuck back into the house in search of cereal and my favorite morning cartoon.

My awareness shifted back to my dark, empty apartment, and sadness overtook me. How had I wandered so very far from that inherent joy that used to be my natural state? Somewhere along the way I'd forgotten how to love and respect myself! Somehow, I'd concluded that control was more important than freedom. Somewhere in there the pure innocent inner joy of childhood had been discounted as the best use of my time.

I sat reveling in this mind-blowing awareness, and saw the lunacy of it all—how unimportant was that which I clung to for dear life! I vowed that day to find my way back to the pure, inner joy I felt as a child. I had no idea how I was going to make my way through the tangled vines and thorny brush of my mind, but now at least I had a beacon, a homing device, to follow.

The Re-Entrance of Joy

My first act of duty was to break the cycle of the bulimia. I felt guided to take a semester in France, a respite from my regular life, in order to begin my healing process. The universe couldn't have arranged it better. Within the close quarters of the French family with whom I stayed, there was no option to miss a meal or to sneak food. The walls were paper thin, so purging afterward was rarely an option.

Also, I was blessed to align with two other young women profoundly comfortable in their curvy bodies of various sizes. They radiated confidence, sexiness, and power, and men responded! Under the loving, supportive energy of these two living angels, I began to see glimmers of what inner confidence and self-love looked like. I couldn't quite fully love myself and my body yet, but I could honor myself enough to begin to eat again at every meal, regardless of how it affected my body size.

When I returned home, I took the next hugely important leap. Despite my inner critic's deep fear of ridicule, I admitted to a few close friends and family that I had an eating disorder and—more importantly and uncomfortably—asked for help.

After a few failed attempts at food addiction groups and traditional therapists, I finally found a really good unconventional therapist who saw through every defense I tried, and cut right to the core of my story. Patty was fierce about self-love and helped me see the value for all involved when I put respecting myself above the approval of others. In that safe container, I was given full permission to let go of control and to express every emotion. For once, I didn't have to be the strong one. How liberating! I peeled away layer after layer of protection, defense, and guilt. It was *extremely* uncomfortable and oh, so liberating!

A lot had to change as I replaced my destructive habits with self-love and self-care. I quit drinking and smoking, released many of my unhealthy relationships, and started eating foods that actually nourished my body. And, equally as important, I began to seek out the kind of deeper nourishment one can never find in a food group.

I found myself in my mother's library one afternoon, browsing titles on personal growth and spirituality, when I happened upon "Conversations with God" by Neale Donald Walsh. Until then, I considered myself an "intellectual agnostic," whose only association with the word "God" was negative.

But something in that book called me, and I was learning to listen to my inner voice. I was astounded at how much of Neale's story and principles in the book resonated with me—despite the fact that his guy thought he was having a conversation with God! Though I still didn't know if I believed in all the "God and spirit stuff" about which he spoke, it did sound like a better way of living than the thinking that had created my previously destructive past.

And so began my spiritual path.

After devouring the "Conversations with God" trilogy, I moved on to don Miguel Ruiz, Byron Katie, and Abraham-Hicks, among others. With the help of these wise teachers of truth, I questioned all the destructive stories I'd been taught by others and began replacing them one-by-one with new, loving, empowering beliefs. I learned to trust my inner voice above all else, applied everything that felt true, and threw out what did not. Over time, the voices of doubt, judgment, and fear began to lessen and the playful joy and freedom that had once been my dominant state began to blossom.

Living in Joy

Fourteen years later, as I sit in my garden on a sunny spring afternoon listening to the wind tinkle through the chimes, I'm happy to say I truly love my life. I feel inner joy on a regular basis and trust completely in the goodness of the universe. I love myself — truly, unconditionally — and have so much more to give to others from that space now. Through my work as a spiritual coach and my role as Course Production Manager at The Shift Network, I'm blessed to provide awakening souls across the world the opportunity to consciously create the life of their dreams—as I did—and to give of their gifts more fully in the world.

I'm not saying I don't have difficult days. There is still learning and growth at every turn. But I can say safely my good days far outweigh my bad, and the more negative times now carry far more richness. I find value in each challenge to help me stretch and grow, and handle the setbacks with greater grace. I feel into the future and sense so much good to come. However, in this moment I'm simply grateful for all the joy, love, and true spiritual nourishment that are right here, right now...

ABOUT THE AUTHOR: Michelle Renee Johnson CEC, PCC is a Spiritual Coach, Speaker, Writer & owner of Expanding Joy Coaching. Michelle specializes in supporting those already powerfully on their spiritual path in creating from and living as their fullest expression so they can provide their unique gifts to the world in the most effective, passionate, joyous way possible. Michelle offers support through one-on-one coaching and workshops, is a monthly columnist for Upbeat Time Magazine and works with many well-known spiritual teachers including Gay Hendricks, Gary Zukav, Thomas Huebl, & don Miguel Ruiz developing and hosting courses for The Shift Network.

Michelle Renee Johnson, CEC, PCC
Certified Empowerment Coach, Spiritual Teacher and Mentor
www.expandingjoycoaching.com
info@expandingjoycoaching.com
916-671-8635

About the Authors

Are you inspired by the stories in this book?
Let the authors know.

See the contact information at the end of each chapter
and reach out to them.

They'd love to hear from you!

Each author in this book retains the copyright and all inherent
rights to her individual chapter. Their stories are printed herein
with each author's permission.

Each author is responsible for the individual opinions expressed
through her words.

Acknowledgements & Gratitude

OUR GRATITUDE overflows to the many incredible women who have come together with such open hearts to lift the world, one woman at a time, to a space of joy, love and possibility.

To the authors of these stories we applaud you, honor you and love you. You exemplify resilience, courage, selflessness and, even more than these, you radiate pure love and the beauty of the human spirit. We are honored to share this journey with you, and so grateful that you stepped fully into your power by offering your own story to light the way for others. You are a beautiful example of love in action.

"It takes a village..." to birth a book and we are so very thankful for our tribe and their guidance, expertise, love and support! To our editor Sheri Horn-Hasan who seems to know just the right questions to ask to get to the heart and essence of the stories; our graphic designer Jodie Penn who artfully 'sees' the perfect cover; and our training team, AmondaRose Igoe, Jennifer Connell and Laura Rubinstein, as well as those who contributed behind the scenes - We love each of you!

Kumari, our dear friend, advisor, enlightened spirit – Your words are a masterpiece of inspired truth to light the way for our authors to shine. Namaste`

To our friends and families, we love you! Your unwavering and loving support of our inspirations and projects continue to allow us to faithfully pursue our passion and vision for life.

Above all, we are grateful for the Divine Spirit that flows through us each day providing continued blessings, lessons and opportunities for growth, peace and JOY!

With much love and deep gratitude,
Sue Urda and Kathy Fyler

About Sue Urda and Kathy Fyler

Sue and Kathy have been friends for 23 years and business partners since 1994. They have received awards and accolades for their businesses over the years and they love their latest foray into book publishing where they provide a forum for women to achieve their dreams of becoming published authors.

Their pride and joy is Powerful You! Women's Network, which they claim is a gift from Spirit. They love traveling the country producing meetings and tour events to gather women for business, personal and spiritual growth. Their greatest pleasure comes through connecting with the many inspiring and extraordinary women who are a part of their network.

The strength of their partnership lies in their deep respect and understanding of one another as well as their complementary skills and knowledge. Kathy is a technology enthusiast and free-thinker. Sue is an author and speaker with a knack for creative undertakings. Their love for each other is boundless.

Together their energies combine to feed the flames of countless women who are seeking truth, empowerment, joy, peace and connection with themselves, their own spirits and other women.

Reach Sue and Kathy:
Powerful You! Inc.
973-248-1262
info@powerfulyou.com
www.powerfulyou.com

Powerful You! Women's Network
Networking with a Heart

OUR MISSION is to empower women to find their inner wisdom, follow their passion and live rich, authentic lives.

Powerful You! Women's Network is founded upon the belief that women are powerful creators, passionate and compassionate leaders, and the heart and backbone of our world's businesses, homes, and communities.

Our Network welcomes all women from all walks of life. We recognize that diversity in our relationships creates opportunities.

Powerful You! creates and facilitates venues for women who desire to develop connections that will assist in growing their businesses. We aid in the creation of lasting personal relationships and provide insights and tools for women who seek balance, grace and ease in all facets of life.

Powerful You! was founded in January 2005 to gather women for business, personal and spiritual growth. Our monthly chapter meetings provide a collaborative and comfortable space for networking, connections and creating personal relationships. Because we know that relationships are built through real and meaningful conversations, our meetings include opportunities for discussions, mini-masterminds, speakers, and gratitude shares.

Follow us online:
Twitter: @powerfulyou
www.facebook.com/powerfulyou

Join or Start a Chapter for
Business, Personal & Spiritual Growth

www.powerfulyou.com

Are You Being Called to Share Your Story?

Would You Like to Contribute to Our Next Inspiring Anthology Book?

If you're like most women, you have a story to tell, but you may find it daunting to even consider writing a whole book on your own. No worries! We're here to help!

If you've always wanted to be an author and can see yourself partnering with other women to share your story, an anthology book is the answer you've been seeking.

We provide complete and personal guidance through the writing and editing process. Our packages include complete publishing services, writing consultation, a bestseller campaign, expert training, author interviews, book marketing tools, lots of exposure, an instant team of co-authors, and of course, books and bookmarks.

We are committed to helping women express their voices and shine their light into the world. Won't you join us? Become an Author with Powerful You! Publishing.

Powerful You!
PUBLISHING
Sharing Wisdom ~ Shining Light

Powerful You! Publishing
973-248-1262
powerfulyoupublishing.com

About Kumari

Internationally acclaimed intuitive healer, author, visionary and animal mystic, Kumari's deepest joy is empowering others to unwrap their innate intuitive, manifesting and healing gifts.

Kumari is the host of "How to Heal Anything" an internet TV program; former host of "Co-Creation Activations" on World Puja, a leading empowerment radio network. She is co-author of the bestselling book "Empowering Transformations for Women." Her transformational work includes critically acclaimed CDs "Connecting with All Life" and "Awaken Your Soul", the groundbreaking "Divine Human" course and Quantum Creating retreats.

Kumari's mission is to inspire awareness and compassion through exploring the human/animal spiritual connection as a vehicle to experience the bliss of Oneness. She serves as a catalyst for global ascension through conscious vibrational healing. She has facilitated thousands of people...and their animal friends in achieving profound transformations.

Kumari holds a palpable energetic presence where healing occurs spontaneously and the light and wisdom of the Soul unveils. She teaches with a practicality and playfulness that is disarmingly potent, fully anchored in the knowing that anyone can awaken to the magical remembrance of their divine nature.

Kumari Mullin
P.O. BOX 1354
Roseland, FL 32957
(772) 589-9803
www.KumariHealing.com